The Vagabond in

Arthur Compton-Rickett

Alpha Editions

This edition published in 2024

ISBN : 9789362090324

Design and Setting By
Alpha Editions
www.alphaedis.com
Email - info@alphaedis.com

As per information held with us this book is in Public Domain.
This book is a reproduction of an important historical work. Alpha Editions uses the best technology to reproduce historical work in the same manner it was first published to preserve its original nature. Any marks or number seen are left intentionally to preserve its true form.

Contents

FOREWORD .... - 1 -
INTRODUCTION .... - 3 -
I WILLIAM HAZLITT .... - 11 -
II THOMAS DE QUINCEY .... - 21 -
III GEORGE BORROW .... - 32 -
IV HENRY D. THOREAU .... - 50 -
V ROBERT LOUIS STEVENSON .... - 65 -
VI RICHARD JEFFERIES .... - 78 -
VII WALT WHITMAN .... - 94 -
BIBLIOGRAPHICAL NOTES .... - 117 -
Footnotes .... - 119 -

FOREWORD

In the introductory paper to this volume an attempt is made to justify the epithet "Vagabond" as applied to writers of a certain temperament. This much may be said here: the term Vagabond is used in no derogatory sense. Etymologically it signifies a wanderer; and such is the meaning attached to the term in the following pages. Differing frequently in character and in intellectual power, a basic similarity of temperament gives the various writers discussed a remarkable spiritual affinity. For in each one the wandering instinct is strong. Sometimes it may take a physical, sometimes an intellectual expression—sometimes both. But always it shows itself, and always it is opposed to the routine and conventions of ordinary life.

These papers are primarily studies in temperament; and the literary aspects have been subordinated to the personal element. In fact, they are studies of certain forces in modern literature, viewed from a special standpoint. And the standpoint adopted may, it is hoped, prove suggestive, though it does not pretend to be exhaustive.

If the papers on Hazlitt and De Quincey are more fragmentary than the others, it is because these writers have been already discussed by the author in a previous volume. It has been thought unnecessary to repeat the points raised there, and these studies may be regarded therefore as at once supplementary and complementary.

My cordial thanks are due to Mr. Theodore Watts-Dunton, who has taken so kindly and friendly an interest in this little volume. He was good enough to read the proofs, and to express his appreciation, especially of the Borrow and Thoreau articles, in most generous terms. I had hoped, indeed, that he would have honoured these slight studies by a prefatory note, and he had expressed a wish to do so. Unhappily, prior claims upon his time prevented this. The book deals largely, it will be seen, with those "Children of the Open Air" about whom the eloquent author of *Aylwin* so often has written. I am especially glad, therefore, to quote (with Mr. Watts-Dunton's permission) his fine sonnet, where the "Vagabond" spirit in its happiest manifestation is expressed.

> "A TALK ON WATERLOO BRIDGE
> "THE LAST SIGHT OF GEORGE BORROW
>
> "We talked of 'Children of the Open Air,'
> Who once on hill and valley lived aloof,
> Loving the sun, the wind, the sweet reproof
> Of storms, and all that makes the fair earth fair,
> Till, on a day, across the mystic bar

Of moonrise, came the 'Children of the Roof,'
Who find no balm 'neath evening's rosiest woof,
Nor dews of peace beneath the Morning Star.
We looked o'er London, where men wither and choke,
Roofed in, poor souls, renouncing stars and skies,
And lore of woods and wild wind prophecies,
Yea, every voice that to their fathers spoke:
And sweet it seemed to die ere bricks and smoke
Leave never a meadow outside Paradise." [0]

A. R.

London, *October*, 1906

INTRODUCTION
THE VAGABOND ELEMENT IN MODERN LITERATURE

> "There's night and day, brother, both sweet things; sun, moon, and stars, brother, all sweet things; there's likewise a wind on the heath."—*Lavengro*.

I

There are some men born with a vagrant strain in the blood, an unsatiable inquisitiveness about the world beyond their doors. Natural revolutionaries they, with an ingrained distaste for the routine of ordinary life and the conventions of civilization. The average common-sense Englishman distrusts the Vagabond for his want of sympathy with established law and order. Eccentricity and unconventionality smack to him always of moral obliquity. And thus it is that the literary Vagabond is looked at askance. One is reminded of Mr. Pecksniff: "Pagan, I regret to state," observed that gentleman of the Sirens on one occasion. Unhappily no one pointed out to this apostle of purity that the naughtiness of the Sirens was not necessarily connected with paganism, and that the siren disposition has been found even "in choirs and places where they sing."

Restlessness, then, is one of the notes of the Vagabond temperament.

Sometimes the Vagabond is a physical, sometimes only an intellectual wanderer; but in any case there is about him something of the primal wildness of the woods and hills.

Thus it is we find in the same spiritual brotherhood men so different in genius and character as Hazlitt, De Quincey, Thoreau, Whitman, Borrow, Jefferies, Stevenson.

Thoreau turned his back on civilization, and found a new joy of living in the woods at Maine. 'Tis the Open Road that inspired Whitman with his rude, melodic chants. Not the ways of men and women, but the flaunting "pageant of summer" unlocked the floodgates of Jefferies' heart. Hazlitt was never so gay, never wrote of books with such relish, as when he was recounting a country walk. There are few more beautiful passages than those where he describes the time when he walked between Wrexham and Llangollen, his imagination aglow with some lines of Coleridge. De Quincey loved the shiftless, nomadic life, and gloried in uncertainties and peradventures. A wandering, open-air life was absolutely indispensable to Borrow's happiness; and Stevenson had a schoolboy's delight in the make-believe of Romance.

II

Another note now discovers itself—a passion for the Earth. All these men had a passion for the Earth, an intense joy in the open air. This feeling differs from the Nature-worship of poets like Wordsworth and Shelly. It is less romantic, more realistic. The attitude is not so much that of the devotee as that of the lover. There is nothing mystical or abstract about it. It is direct, personal, intimate. I call it purposely a passion for the Earth rather than a passion for Nature, in order to distinguish it from the pronounced transcendentalism of the romantic poets.

The poet who has expressed most nearly the attitude of these Vagabonds towards Nature—more particularly that of Thoreau, Whitman, Borrow, and Jefferies—is Mr. George Meredith.

Traces of it may be found in Browning with reference to the "old brown earth," and in William Morris, who exclaimed—

"My love of the earth and the worship of it!"

but Mr. Meredith has given the completest expression to this Earth-worship.

One thinks of Thoreau and Jefferies when reading Melampus—

"With love exceeding a simple love of the things
That glide in grasses and rubble of woody wreck;
Or change their perch on a beat of quivering wings
From branch to branch, only restful to pipe and peck;
Or, bristled, curl at a touch their snouts in a ball;
Or, cast their web between bramble and thorny hook;
The good physician Melampus, loving them all,
Among them walked, as a scholar who reads a book."

While that ripe oddity, "Juggling Jerry," would have delighted the "Romany"-loving Borrow.

Indeed the Nature philosophy of Mr. Meredith, with its virile joy in the rich plenitude of Nature and its touch of wildness has more in common with Thoreau, with Jefferies, with Borrow, and with Whitman than with Wordsworth, Coleridge, Shelley, or even with Tennyson—the first of our poets to look upon the Earth with the eyes of the scientist.

III

But a passion for the Earth is not sufficient of itself to admit within the charmed circle of the Vagabond; for there is no marked restlessness about Mr. Meredith's genius, and he lacks what it seems to me is the third note of the genuine literary Vagabond—the note of aloofness, of personal detachment. This it is which separates the Vagabond from the generality of his fellows. No very prolonged scrutiny of the disposition of Thoreau, Jefferies, and Borrow is needed to reveal a pronounced shyness and reserve. Examine this trait more closely, and it will exhibit a certain emotional coldness towards the majority of men and women. No one can overlook the chill austerity that marks Thoreau's attitude in social converse. Borrow, again, was inaccessible to a degree, save to one or two intimates; even when discovered among congenial company, with the gipsies or with companions of the road like Isopel Berners, exhibiting, to me, a genial bleakness that is occasionally exasperating.

It was his constitutional reserve that militated against the success of Jefferies as a writer. He was not easy to get on with, not over fond of his kind, and rarely seems quite at ease save in the solitude of the fields.

Whitman seems at first sight an exception. Surely here was a friendly man if ever there was one. Yet an examination of his life and writings will compel us to realize a lack of deep personal feeling in the man. He loves the People rather than the people. Anyone who will go along with him is a welcome comrade. This catholic spirit of friendliness is delightful and attractive in many ways, but it has its drawbacks; it is not possible perhaps to have both extensity and intensity of emotion. There is the impartial friendliness of the wind and sun about his salutations. He loves all men—because they are a part of Nature; but it is the common human element in men and women themselves that attracts him. There was less of the Ishmaelite about Whitman than about Thoreau, Borrow, or Jefferies; but the man whose company he really delighted in was the "powerful, uneducated man"—the artisan and the mechanic. Those he loved best were those who had something of the elemental in their natures—those who lived nearest to the earth. Without denying for a moment that Whitman was capable of genuine affection, I cannot help feeling, from the impression left upon me by his writings, and by accounts given by those who knew him, that what I must call an absence of human *passion*—not necessarily affection—which seems to characterize more or less the Vagabond generally, may be detected in Whitman, no less than in Thoreau and Borrow. It would seem that the passion for the earth, which made them—to use one of Mr. Watts-Dunton's happy phrases—"Children of the Open Air," took the place of a passion for human kind.

In the papers dealing with these writers these points are discussed at greater length. For the present reference is made to them in order to illustrate the characteristics of the Vagabond temperament, and to vindicate my generic title.

The characteristics, then, which I find in the Vagabond temperament are (1) Restlessness—the wandering instinct; this expresses itself mentally as well as physically. (2) A passion for the Earth—shown not only in the love of the open air, but in a delight in all manifestations of life. (3) A constitutional reserve whereby the Vagabond, though rejoicing in the company of a few kindred souls, is put out of touch with the majority of men and women. This is a temperamental idiosyncrasy, and must not be confounded with misanthropy.

These characteristics are not found in equal degree among the writers treated of in these pages. Sometimes one predominates, sometimes another. That is to be expected. But to some extent all these characteristics prevail.

IV

There is a certain type of Vagabondage which may be covered by the term "Bohemianism." But 'tis of a superficial character mostly, and is in the nature of a town-made imitation. Graces and picturesqueness it may have of a kind, but it lacks the rough virility, the sturdy grit, which is the most attractive quality of the best Vagabond.

Bohemianism indeed is largely an attitude of dress; Vagabondage an attitude of spirit. At heart the Bohemian is not really unconventional; he is not nomadic by instinct as is the Vagabond.

Take the case of Charles Lamb. There was a man whose habits of life were pleasantly Bohemian, and whose sympathy with the Vagabond temperament has made some critics over-hastily class him temperamentally with writers like Hazlitt and De Quincey. He was not a true Vagabond at all. He was a Bohemian of the finer order, and his graces of character need no encomium to-day. But he was certainly not a Vagabond. At heart he was devoted to convention. When released from his drudgery of clerkship he confessed frankly how potent an influence routine had been and still was in his life. This is not the tone of the Vagabond. Even Elia's wanderings on paper are more apparent than real, and there is a method in his quaintest fantasies. His discursive essays are arabesques observing geometrical patterns, and though seemingly careless, follow out cunningly preconceived designs. He only appears to digress; but all his bypaths lead back into the high road. Hazlitt, on the other hand, was a genuine digressionalist; so was De Quincey; so was Borrow. There is all the difference between their literary mosaic and the arabesques of Lamb. And should one still doubt how to classify Elia, one could scarcely place him among the "Children of the Open Air." Make what allowance you like for his whimsical remarks about the country, it is certain that no passion for the Earth possessed him.

One characteristic, however, both the Bohemian and the Vagabond have in common—that is, restlessness. And although there is a restlessness which is the outcome of superabundant nervous energy—the restlessness of Dickens in his earlier years, for instance—yet it must be regarded as, for the most part, a pathological sign. One of the legacies of the Industrial Revolution has been the neurotic strain which it has bequeathed to our countrymen. The stress of life upon the nervous system in this era of commercialism has produced a spirit of feverish unrest which, permeating society generally, has visited a few souls with special intensity. It has never been summed up better than by Ruskin, when, in one of his scornful flashes, he declared that our two objects in life were: whatever we have, to get more; and wherever we are, to go somewhere else. Nervous instability is very marked in the case of Hazlitt and De Quincey; and there was a strain of morbidity in Borrow, Jefferies, and Stevenson.

Far more pronounced in its neurotic character is Modern Bohemianism—as I prefer to call the "town Vagabond." The decadent movement in literature has produced many interesting artistic figures, but they lack the grit and the sanity of outlook which undoubtedly marks the Vagabond. In France to-day morbidity and Vagabondage are inseparable.

Gallic Vagabonds, such as Verlaine and Baudelaire, interesting as they are to men of letters and students of psychology, do not engage our affections as do the English Vagabonds. We do not take kindly to their personalities. It is like passing through the hot streets after inhaling the scent of the woodland. There is something stifling and unhealthy about the atmosphere, and one turns with relief to the vagabondage of men like Whitman, who are "enamoured of growth out of doors."

Of profounder interest is the Russian Vagabond. In Russian Literature the Vagabond seems to be the rule, not the exception.

Every great Russian writer has more or less of the Vagabond about him. Tolstoy, it is true, wears the robe of the Moralist, and Tolstoy the Ascetic cries down Tolstoy the Artist. But I always feel that the most enduring part of Tolstoy's work is the work of the Vagabond temperament that lurks beneath the stern preacher. Political and social exigencies have driven him to take up a position which is certainly not in harmony with many traits in his nature.

In the case of Gorky, of course, we have the Vagabond naked and unashamed. His novels are fervent defences of the Vagabond. What could be franker than this?—"I was born outside society, and for that reason I cannot take in a strong dose of its culture, without soon feeling forced to get outside it again, to wipe away the infinite complications, the sickly refinements, of that kind of existence. I like either to go about in the meanest streets of towns, because, though everything there is dirty, it is all simple and sincere; or else to wander about in the high roads and across the fields, because that is always interesting; it refreshes one morally, and needs no more than a pair of good legs to carry one." Racial differences mark off in many ways the Russian Vagabond from his English brother; a strange fatalism, a fierce melancholy, and a nature of greater emotional intensity; but in the passage quoted how much in common they have also.

V

There were literary Vagabonds in England before the nineteenth century. Many interesting and picturesque figures—Marlowe's, for instance—arrest the attention of the student, and to some extent the characteristics noted may be traced in these. But every century, no less than every country, has its psychological atmosphere, and the modern literary Vagabond is quite a distinctive individual. Some I know are inclined to regard Goldsmith as one of the Vagabond band; but, although a charming Vagabond in many ways, he did not express his Vagabondage in his writings. The spirit of his time was not conducive to Vagabond literature. The spirit of the succeeding age especially favoured the Vagabond strain.

The Gothic Revival, and the newly-awakened interest in medievalism, warmed the imaginations of verse men and prose men alike. The impulse to wander, to scale some "peak in Darien" for the joy of a "wild surmise," seized every artist in letters—poet, novelist, essayist. A longing for the mystic world, a passion for the unknown, surged over men's minds with the same power and impetuosity as it had done in the days of the Renaissance. Ordinary life had grown uglier, more sordid; life seemed crushed in the thraldom of mechanism. Men felt like schoolboys pent up in a narrow whitewashed room who look out of the windows at the smiling and alluring world beyond the gates. Small wonder that some who hastened to escape should enter more thoroughly than more cautious souls into the unconventional and the changeful.

The swing of the pendulum was sure to come, and it is not surprising that the mid-century furnishes fewer instances of literary Vagabonds and of Vagabond moods. But with the pre-Raphaelite Movement an impulse towards Vagabondage revived. And the era which started with a De Quincey closed with a Stevenson.

VI

Many writers who cannot be classed among the Vagabonds gave occasional expression to the Vagabond moods which sweep across every artist's soul at some time or other. It would be beside my purpose to dwell at length upon these Vagabond moods, for my chief concern is with the thorough-going wanderer. Mention may be made in passing, however, of Robert Browning, whose cordial detestation of Bohemianism is so well known. Outwardly there was far less of the Vagabond about him than about Tennyson. However the romantic spirit may have touched his boyhood and youth, there looked little of it in the staid, correctly dressed, middle-aged gentleman who attended social functions and cheerfully followed the life conventional. One recalls his disgust with George Sand and her Bohemian circle, his hatred for spiritualism, his almost Philistine horror of the shiftless and lawless elements in life. At the same time I feel that Mr. Chesterton, in his brilliant monograph of the poet, has overstated the case when he says that "neither all his liberality nor all his learning ever made him anything but an Englishman of the middle class." He had mixed blood in his veins, and the fact that his grandmother was a Creole is not to be lightly brushed aside by a Chestertonian paradox. For the Southern blood shows itself from time to time in an unmistakable manner. It is all very well to say that "he carried the prejudices of his class (i.e. the middle class) into eternity!" But we have to reckon with the hot passion of "Time's Revenges," the daring unconventionality of "Fifine at the Fair," and the rare sympathy and discernment of the gipsy temperament in "The Flight of the Duchess." Conventional prejudices Browning undoubtedly had, and there was a splendid level-headedness about the man which kept in check the extravagances of Vagabondage.

But no poet who has studied men and women as he had studied them, pondering with loving care the curious, the complex, the eccentric, could have failed to break away at times from the outlook of the middle-class Englishman.

Tennyson, on the other hand, looking the handsome Vagabond to the life, living apart from the world, as if its conventions and routine were distasteful to him, had scarcely a touch of the Vagabond in his temperament. That he had no Vagabond moods I will not say; for the poet who had no Vagabond moods has yet to be born. But he frowned them down as best he could, and in his writings we can see the typical, cultured, middle-class Englishman as we certainly fail to see in Browning. A great deal of Tennyson is merely Philistinism made musical. The romantic temper scarcely touches him at all; and in those noble poems—"Lucretius," "Ulysses," "Tithonus"—where his special powers find their happiest expression, the attitude of mind has nothing in common with that of the Vagabond. It was classic art, not romantic art, that attracted Tennyson.

Compare the "Guinevere" of Tennyson with the "Guenevere" of Morris, and you realize at once the vast difference that separates Sentimentalism from Romanticism. And Vagabondage can be approached only through the gateway of Romanticism.

VII

In looking back upon these discursive comments on the Vagabond element in modern literature, one cannot help asking what is the resultant effect of the Vagabond temperament upon life and thought. As psychologists no doubt we are content to examine its peculiarities and extravagances without troubling to ask how far it has made for sanity and sweetness.

Yet the question sooner or later rises to our lips. This Vagabond temperament—is its charm and attractiveness merely superficial? I cannot think so. I think that on the whole its effect upon our literature has been salutary and beneficial.

These more eager, more adventurous spirits express for us the holiday mood of life. For they are young at heart, inasmuch as they have lived in the sunshine, and breathed in the fresh, untainted air. They have indeed scattered "a new roughness and gladness" among men and women, for they have spoken to us of the simple magic of the Earth.

I
WILLIAM HAZLITT

"He that is weary, let him sit,
  My soul would stir
And trade in courtesies and wit,
  Quitting the fur
To cold complexions needing it."

GEORGE HERBERT.

"Men of the world, who know the world like men,
Who think of something else beside the pen."

BYRON.

I

It is not unusual to hear the epithet "complex" flung with a too ready alacrity at any character who evinces eccentricity of disposition. In olden days, when regularity of conduct, and conformity even in small particulars were regarded as moral essentials, the eccentric enjoyed short shrift. The stake, the guillotine, or the dungeons of the Inquisition speedily put an end to the eccentricities. A slight measure of nonconformity was quite enough to earn the appellation of witch or wizard. One stood no chance as an eccentric unless the eccentricity was coupled with unusual force of character.

Alienists assure us that insanity is on the increase, and it is certain that modern conditions of life have favoured nervous instabilities of temperament, which express themselves in eccentricities of conduct. But nervous instability is one thing, complexity another. The fact that they may co-exist affords us no excuse for confusing them. We speak of a man's personality, whereas it would be more correct to speak of his personalities.

Much has been written of late years about multi-personalities, until the impression has spread that the possession of a number of differing personalities is a special form of insanity. This is quite wrong. The sane, no less than the insane man has a number of personalities, and the difference between them lies in the power of co-ordination. The sane man is like a skilful driver who is able to control his team of horses; whereas the insane man has lost control of his steeds, and allows first one and then the other to get the mastery of him.

The personalities are no more numerous than before, only we are made aware of their number.

In a sense, therefore, every human being is complex. Inheritance and environment have left distinctive characteristics, which, if the power of co-ordination be weakened, take possession of the individual as opportunity may determine. We usually apply the term personality to the resulting blend of the various personalities in his nature. In the case of sane men and women the personality is a very composite affair. What we are thinking of frequently when we apply the epithet "complex" is a certain contradictoriness of temperament, the result of opposing strains of blood. It is the quality, not the quantities, of the personalities that affects us. If not altogether happy, the expression may in these cases pass as a rough indication of the opposing element in their nature. But when used, as it often is, merely to indicate an eccentricity, the epithet assumes a restricted significance. A may be far more complex than B; but his power of co-ordination, what we call his will, is strong, whereas that of B is weak, so we reserve the term complex for the weaker individual. But why reserve the term complex for a few literary decadents who have lost the power of co-ordination, and not apply it to a mind like Shakespeare's, who was certainly as complex a personality as ever lived?

Now I do not deny that it is wrong to apply the term complexity to men of unstable, nervous equilibrium. What I do deny is the right to apply the term to these men only, thus disseminating the fallacy—too popular nowadays—that genius and insanity are inseparable.

As a matter of fact, if we turn to Spencer's exposition of the evolutionary doctrine we shall find an illustration ready at hand to show that complexity is of two kinds. Evolution, as he tells us, is a change from homogeneity to heterogeneity, from a simple to a complex. Thus a dog is more complex than a dog-fish, a man than a dog, a Shakespeare greater than a Shaw. But complexity, though a law of Evolution, is not *the* law of Evolution. Mere complexity is not necessarily a sign of a higher organism. It may be induced by injury, as, for instance, the presence of a marked growth such as cancer. Here we have a more complex state, but complexity of this kind is on the road to dissolution and disintegration. Cancer, in fact, in the body is like disaffection in an army. The unity is disturbed and differences are engendered. Thus, given a measure of nervous instability, a complexity may be induced, a disintegration of the composite personality into the various separate personalities, that bespeaks a lower, not a higher organism. [21]

Now all this may seem quite impertinent to our subject, but I have discussed the point at length because complexity is certainly one of the marks of the Vagabond, and it is important to make quite clear what is connoted by that term.

Recognizing, then, the two types of complexity, the type of complexity with which I am concerned especially in these papers is the higher type. I have not selected these writers merely on account of their eccentricities or deviations from the normal. Mere eccentricity has a legitimate interest for the scientist, but for the psychologist it is of no particular moment. Hazlitt is not interesting *because* he was afflicted with a morbid egotism; or Borrow *because* he suffered from fits of melancholia; or De Quincey *because* he imagined he was in debt when he had plenty of money. It was because these neurotic signs were associated with powerful intellects and exceptional imaginations, and therefore gave a peculiar and distinctive character to their writings—in short, because they happened to be men of genius, men of higher complex organisms than the average individual—that they interest so strongly.

It seems to me a kind of inverted admiration that is attracted to what is bizarre and out of the way, and confounds peculiarity with cleverness and eccentricity with genius.

The real claim that individuals have upon our appreciation and sympathy is mental and moral greatness; and the sentimental weakness with the "oddity" is no more rational, no more to be respected, than a sympathy which extends to physical monstrosities and sees nothing to admire in a normal, healthy body.

It may be urged, of course, by some that I have admitted to a neurotic strain affecting more or less all the Vagabonds treated of in this volume, and this being so, it is clear that the morbid tendencies in their temperament must have conditioned the distinctive character of their genius.

Now it is quite true that the soil whence the flower of their genius sprung was in several cases not without a taint; but it does not follow that the flower itself is tainted. And here we come upon the fallacy that seems to me to lie at the basis of the doctrine which makes genius itself a kind of disease. The soil of the rose garden may be manured with refuse that Nature uses in bringing forth the lovely bloom of the rose. But the poisonous character of the refuse has been chemically transformed in giving vitality to the roses. And so from unhealthy stock, from temperaments affected by disease, have sprung the roses of genius—transformed by the mysterious alchemy of the imagination into pure and lovely things. There are, of course, poisonous flowers, just as there is a type of genius—not the highest type—that is morbid. But this does not affect my contention that genius is not necessarily morbid because it may have sprung from a morbid soil. Hazlitt is a case in point. His temperament was certainly not free from morbidity, and this morbidity may be traced in his writings. The most signal instance is the *Liber Amoris*—an unfortunate chapter of sentimental autobiography which did irreparable mischief to his reputation. But there is nothing morbid in Hazlitt at his best; and let it be added that the bulk of Hazlitt's writings displays a noble sanity.

Much has been written about his less pleasing idiosyncrasies, and no writer has been called more frequently to account for deficiencies. It is time surely that we should recall once more the tribute of Lamb: "I think William Hazlitt to be in his natural and healthy state one of the wisest and finest spirits breathing."

II

The complexity of Hazlitt's temperament was especially emphasized by the two strong, opposing tendencies that called for no ordinary power of co-ordination. I mean the austere, individualistic, Puritan strain that came from his Presbyterian forefathers; and a sensuous, voluptuous strain that often ran athwart his Puritanism and occasioned him many a mental struggle. The general effect of these two dements in his nature was this: In matters of the intellect the Puritan was uppermost; in the realm of the emotions you felt the dominant presence of the opposing element.

In his finest essays one feels the presence at once of the Calvinist and the Epicurean; not as two incompatibles, but as opposing elements that have blent together into a noble unity; would-be rivals that have co-ordinated so that from each the good has been extracted, and the less worthy sides eliminated. Thus the sweetness of the one and the strength of the other have combined to give more distinction and power to the utterance.

Take this passage from one of his lectures:—

> "The poet of nature is one who, from the elements of beauty, of power, and of passion in his own breast, sympathises with whatever is beautiful, and grand, and impassioned in nature, in its simple majesty, in its immediate appeal to the senses, to the thoughts and hearts of all men; so that the poet of nature, by the truth, and depth, and harmony of his mind, may be said to hold communion with the very soul of nature; to be identified with, and to foreknow, and to record, the feelings of all men, at all times and places, as they are liable to the same impressions; and to exert the same power over the minds of his readers that nature does. He sees things in their eternal beauty, for he sees them as they are; he feels them in their universal interest, for he feels them as they affect the first principles of his and our common nature. Such was Homer, such was Shakespeare, whose works will last as

long as nature, because they are a copy of the indestructible forms and everlasting impulses of feature, welling out from the bosom as from a perennial spring, or stamped upon the senses by the hand of their Maker. The power of the imagination in them is the representative power of all nature. It has its centre in the human soul, and makes the circuit of the universe."

And this:—

"The child is a poet, in fact, when he first plays at hide-and-seek, or repeats the story of Jack the Giant-killer; the shepherd boy is a poet when he first crowns his mistress with a garland of flowers; the countryman when he stops to look at the rainbow; the city apprentice when he gazes after the Lord Mayor's show; the miser when he hugs his gold; the courtier who builds his hopes upon a smile; the savage who paints his idol with blood; the slave who worships a tyrant, or the tyrant who fancies himself a god; the vain, the ambitious, the proud, the choleric man, the hero and the coward, the beggar and the king, the rich and the poor, the young and the old, all live in a world of their own making; and the poet does no more than describe what all the others think and act."

"Poetry is not a branch of authorship; it is the stuff of which our life is made."

The artist is speaking in Hazlitt, but beneath the full, rich exuberance of the artist, you can detect an under-note of austerity.

Then again, his memorable utterance about the Dissenting minister from one of his essays on "Court Influence."

"A Dissenting minister is a character not so easily to be dispensed with, and whose place cannot be well supplied. It is a pity that this character has worn itself out; that that pulse of thought and feeling has ceased almost to beat in the heart of a nation, who, if not remarkable for sincerity and plain downright well-meaning, are remarkable for nothing. But we have known some such, in happier days, who had been brought up and lived from youth to age in the one constant belief in God and of His Christ, and who thought all other things but dross compared with the glory hereafter to be revealed. Their youthful hopes and vanity had been mortified in them, even in their boyish days, by the neglect and supercilious regards of the world; and they turned to look into their own minds for something else to build their hopes and confidence upon. They were true priests. They set up an image in their own minds—it was truth; they worshipped an idol there—it was justice. They looked on man as their brother, and only bowed the knee to the Highest. Separate from the world, they walked humbly with their God, and lived in thought with those who had borne testimony of a good conscience, with the spirits of just men in all ages.... Their sympathy was not with the oppressors, but the oppressed. They cherished in their thoughts—and wished to transmit to their posterity—those rights and privileges for asserting which their ancestors had bled on scaffolds, or had pined in dungeons, or in foreign climes. Their creed, too, was 'Glory to God, peace on earth, goodwill to man.' This creed, since profaned and rendered vile, they kept fast through good report and evil report. This belief they had, that looks at something out of itself, fixed as the stars, deep as the firmament; that makes of its own heart an altar to truth, a place of worship for what is right, at which it does reverence with praise and prayer like a holy thing, apart and content; that feels that the greatest Being in the universe is always near it; and that all things work together for the good of His creatures, under His guiding hand. This covenant they kept, as the stars keep their courses; this principle they stuck by, for want of knowing better, as it sticks by them to the last. It grows with their growth, it does not wither in their decay. It lives when the almond-tree flourishes, and is not bowed down with the tottering knees. It glimmers with the last feeble eyesight, smiles in the faded cheek like infancy, and lights a path before them to the grave!"

Here is a man of Puritan lineage speaking; but is it the voice of Puritanism only? Surely it is a Puritanism softened and refined, a Puritanism which is free of those harsh and unpleasing elements that have too often obscured its finer aspects. I know of no passage in his writings which for spacious eloquence, nobleness of thought, beauty of expression, can rival this. It was written in 1818, when Hazlitt was forty years old, and in the plenitude of his powers.

III

But the power of co-ordination was not always exerted; perhaps not always possible. Had it been so, then Hazlitt would not take his place in this little band of literary Vagabonds.

There are times when the Puritan element disappears; and it is Hazlitt the eager, curious taster of life that is presented to us. For there was the restless inquisitiveness of the Vagabond about him. This gives such delightful piquancy to many of his utterances. He ranges far and wide, and is willing to go anywhere for a fresh sensation that may add to the interest of his intellectual life. He has no patience with readers who will not quit their own small back gardens. He is for ranging "over the hills and far away."

No sympathy he with the readers who take timid constitutionals in literature, choosing only the well-worn paths. He is a true son of the road; the world is before him, and high roads and byways, rough paths and smooth paths, are equally acceptable, provided they add to his zest and enjoyment.

Not that he cares for the new merely because it is new. The essay on "Reading Old Books" is proof enough of that. A literary ramble must not merely be novel, it must have some element of beauty about it, or he will revisit the old haunts of whose beauty he has full cognizance.

The passion for the Earth which was noted as one of the Vagabond's characteristics is not so pronounced in Hazlitt and De Quincey as with the later Vagabonds. But it is unmistakable all the same. There are, he says, "only three pleasures in life pure and lasting, and all derived from inanimate things—books, pictures, and the face of Nature." The somewhat curious use of the word "inanimate" here as applied to the "face of Nature" scarcely does justice to his intense, vivid appreciation of the life of the open air; but at any rate it differentiates his attitude towards Nature from that of Wordsworth and his school. It is a feeling more direct, more concrete, more personal.

He has no special liking for country people. On the contrary, he thinks them a dull, heavy class of people.

"All country people hate one another," he says. "They have so little comfort that they envy their neighbours the smallest pleasure and advantage, and nearly grudge themselves the necessaries of life. From not being accustomed to enjoyment, they become hardened and averse to it—stupid, for want of thought, selfish, for want of society."

No; it is the sheer joy of being in the open, and learning what Whitman called the "profound lesson of reception," that attracted Hazlitt. "What I like best," he declares, "is to lie whole mornings on a sunny bank on Salisbury Plain, without any object before me, neither knowing nor caring how time passes, and thus, 'with light-winged toys and feathered idleness, to melt down hours to moments.'" A genuine Vagabond mood this.

Hazlitt, like De Quincey, had felt the glamour of the city as well as the glamour of the country; not with the irresistibility of Lamb, but for all that potently. But an instinct for the open, the craving for pleasant spaces, and the longing of the hard-driven journalist for the gracious leisure of the country, these things were paramount with both Hazlitt and De Quincey.

In Hazlitt's case there is a touch of wildness, a more primal delight in the roughness and solitude of country places than we find in De Quincey.

"One of the pleasantest things," says Hazlitt, in true Vagabond spirit, "is going on a journey; but I like to go by myself."

The last touch is not only characteristic of Hazlitt, it touches that note of reserve verging on anti-social sentiment that was mentioned as characteristic of the Vagabond.

He justifies his feeling thus with an engaging frankness: "The soul of a journey is liberty, perfect liberty, to think, feel. Do just as one pleases. We go a journey chiefly to be free of all impediments and of all inconveniences; to leave ourselves behind; much more to get rid of others. . . . It is hard if I cannot start some game on these lone heaths. I laugh, I run, I leap, I sing for joy. From the point of yonder rolling cloud I plunge into my past being, and revel there, as the sunburnt Indian plunges headlong into the wave that wafts him to his native shore. Then long-forgotten things, like 'sunken wrack and sunless treasures,' burst upon my eager sight, and I begin to feel, think, and be myself again."

IV

Taken on the whole, the English literary Vagabond is a man of joy, not necessarily a cheerful man. There is a deeper quality about joy than about cheerfulness. Cheerfulness indeed is almost entirely a physical idiosyncrasy. It lies on the surface. A man, serious and silent, may be a joyful man; he can scarcely be a cheerful man. Moody as he was at times, sour-tempered and whimsical as he could be, yet there was a fine quality of joy about Hazlitt. It is this quality of joy that gives the sparkle and relish to his essays. He took the same joy in his books as in his walks, and he communicates this joy to the reader. He appears misanthropic at times, and rages violently at the world; but 'tis merely a passing gust of feeling, and when over, it is easy to see how superficial it was, so little is his general attitude affected by it.

The joyfulness of the Vagabond is no mere light-hearted, graceful spirit. It is of a hardy and virile nature—a quality not to be crushed by misfortune or sickness. Outwardly, neither the lives of Hazlitt nor De Quincey were what we would call happy. Both had to fight hard against adverse fates for many years; both had delicate constitutions, which entailed weary and protracted periods of feeble health.

But there was a fundamental serenity about them. At the end of a hard and fruitless struggle with death, Hazlitt murmured, "Well, I've had a happy life." De Quincey at the close of his long and varied life showed the same tranquil stoicism that had carried him through his many difficulties.

Joyfulness permeates Thoreau's philosophy of life; and until his system was shattered by a painful and incurable complaint, Jefferies had the same splendid capacity for enjoyment, a huge satisfaction in noting the splendour and rich plenitude of the Earth. Whitman's fine optimism defied every attack from without and within; and the deliberate happiness of Stevenson, when temptation to despondency was so strong, is one of his most attractive characteristics.

Yet the characteristic belongs to the English race, and it is quite other with the Russian. Melancholy in his cast of thought, and pessimistic in his philosophy, the Russian Vagabond presents a striking contrast in this particular.

V

Comparing the styles of Hazlitt and De Quincey, one is struck with the greater fire and vigour of Hazlitt.

Indeed, the term which De Quincey applied to certain of his writings—"impassioned prose"—is really more applicable to many of Hazlitt's essays. The dream fugues of De Quincey are delicately imaginative, but real passion is absent from them. The silvery, far-away tones of the opium-eater do not suggest passion.

Besides, an elaborate, involved style such as his does not readily convey passion of any kind. It moves along too slowly, at too leisurely a pace. On the other hand, the prose of Hazlitt was very frequently literally "impassioned." It was sharp, concise, the sentences rang out resolutely and clearly. And no veil of phantasy hung at these times between himself and the object of his description, as with De Quincey, muffling the voice and blurring the vision. Defects it had, which there is no necessity to dwell on here, but there was a passion in Hazlitt's nature and writings which we do not find in his contemporary.

Trying beyond doubt as was the wayward element in Hazlitt's disposition, to his friends it is not without its charm as a literary characteristic. His bitterness against Coleridge in his later years leads him to dwell the longer upon the earlier meetings, upon the Coleridge of Wem and Nether Stowey, and thus his very prejudices leave his readers frequently as gainers.

A passing whim, a transient resentment, will be the occasion of some finely discursive essay on abstract virtues and vices. And, after all, there is at bottom such noble enthusiasm in the man, and where his subjects were not living people, and his judgment is not blinded by some small prejudices, how fair, how just, how large and admirable his view. His faults and failings were of such a character as to bring upon the owner their own retribution. He paid heavily for his mistakes. His splenetic moods and his violent dislikes arose not from a want of sensibility, but from an excess of sensibility. So I do not think they need seriously disturb us. After all, the dagger he uses as a critic is uncommonly like a stage weapon, and does no serious damage.

Better even than his brilliant, suggestive, if capricious, criticisms are his discursive essays on men and things. These abound in a tonic wisdom, a breadth of imagination as welcome as they are rare.

II
THOMAS DE QUINCEY

"In thoughts from the visions of the night when deep sleep falleth on men."—JOB.

I

Although a passion for the Earth is a prevalent note in the character of the literary Vagabond, yet while harking to the call of the country, he is by no means deaf to the call of the town. With the exception of Thoreau, who seemed to have been insensible to any magic save that of the road and woodland, our literary Vagabonds have all felt and confessed to the spell of the city. It was not, as in the case of Lamb and Dickens, the one compelling influence, but it was an influence of no small potency.

The first important event in De Quincey's life was the roaming life on the hillside of North Wales; the second, the wanderings in "stony-hearted Oxford Street." Later on the spell of London faded away, and a longing for the country possessed him once more. But the spell of London was important in shaping his literary life, and must not be underestimated. Mention has been made of Lamb and Dickens, to whom the life of the town meant so much, and whose inspiration they could not forgo without a pang. But these men were not attracted in the same way as De Quincey. What drew De Quincey to London was its mystery; whereas it was the stir and colour of the crowded streets that stirred the imagination of the two Charles's. We scarcely realize as we read of those harsh experiences, those bitter struggles with poverty and loneliness, that the man is writing of his life in London, is speaking of some well-known thoroughfares. It is like viewing a familiar scene in the moonlight, when all looks strange and weird. A faint but palpable veil of phantasy seemed to shut off De Quincey from the outside world. In his most poignant passages the voice has a ghostly ring; in his most realistic descriptions there is a dreamlike unreality. A tender and sensitive soul in his dealings with others, there are no tears in his writings. One has only to compare the early recorded struggles of Dickens with those of De Quincey to feel the difference between the two temperaments. The one passionately concrete, the other dispassionately abstract. De Quincey will take some heartfelt episode and deck it out in so elaborate a panoply of rhetoric that the human element seems to have vanished. Beautiful as are many of the passages describing the pathetic outcast Ann, the reader is too conscious of the stylist and the full-dress stylist.

That he feels what he is writing of, one does not doubt; but he does not suit his manner to his matter. For expressing subtle emotions, half shades of thought, no writer is more wonderfully adept than De Quincey. But when the episode demands simple and direct treatment his elaborate cadences feel out of place.

When he pauses in his description to apostrophize, then the disparity affects one far less; as, for instance, in this apostrophe to "noble-minded" Ann after recalling how on one occasion she had saved his life.

> "O youthful benefactress! how often in succeeding years, standing in solitary places, and thinking of thee with grief of heart and perfect love—how often have I wished that, as in ancient times the curse of a father was believed to have a supernatural power, and to pursue its object with a fatal necessity of self-fulfilment, even so the benediction of a heart oppressed with gratitude might have a like prerogative; might have power given it from above to chase, to haunt, to waylay, to pursue thee into the central darkness of a London brothel, or (if it were possible) even into the darkness of the grave, there to awaken thee with an authentic message of peace and forgiveness, and of final reconciliation!"

Perhaps the passage describing how he befriended the small servant girl in the half-deserted house in Greek Street is among the happiest, despite a note of artificiality towards the close:—

> "Towards nightfall I went down to Greek Street, and found, on taking possession of my new quarters, that the house already contained one single inmate—a poor, friendless child, apparently ten years old; but she seemed hunger-bitten; and sufferings of that sort often make children look older than they are. From this forlorn child I learned that she had slept and lived there alone for some time before I came; and great joy the poor creature expressed when she

found that I was in future to be her companion through the hours of darkness. The house could hardly be called large—that is, it was not large on each separate storey; but, having four storeys in all, it was large enough to impress vividly the sense of its echoing loneliness; and, from the want of furniture, the noise of the rats made a prodigious uproar on the staircase and hall; so that, amidst the real fleshly ills of cold and hunger, the forsaken child had found leisure to suffer still more from the self-created one of ghosts. Against these enemies I could promise her protection; human companionship was in itself protection; but of other and more needful aid I had, alas! little to offer. We lay upon the floor, with a bundle of law papers for a pillow, but with no other covering than a large horseman's cloak; afterwards, however, we discovered in a garret an old sofa-cover, a small piece of rug, and some fragments of other articles, which added a little to our comfort. The poor child crept close to me for warmth, and for security against her ghostly enemies.... Apart from her situation, she was not what would be called an interesting child. She was neither pretty, nor quick in understanding, nor remarkably pleasing in manners. But, thank God! even in those years I needed not the embellishments of elegant accessories to conciliate my affections. Plain human nature, in its humblest and most homely apparel, was enough for me; and I loved the child because she was my partner in wretchedness."

II

I cannot agree with Mr. H. S. Salt when, in the course of a clever and interesting biographical study of De Quincey, [40] he says: "It (in *re* style) conveys precisely the sense that is intended, and attains its effect far less by rhetorical artifice than by an almost faultless instinct in the choice and use of words."

In the delineation of certain moods he is supremely excellent. But surely the style is not a plastic style; and its appeal to the ear rather than to the pictorial faculty limits its emotional effect upon the reader. Images pass before his eyes, and he tries to depict them by cunningly devised phrases; but the veil of phantasy through which he sees those images has blurred their outline and dimmed their colouring. The phrase arrests by its musical cadences, by its solemn, mournful music. Even some of his most admirable pieces—the dream fugues, leave the reader dissatisfied, when they touch poignant realities like sorrow. Despite its many beauties, that dream fugue, "Our Ladies of

Sorrow," seems too misty, too ethereal in texture for the intense actuality of the subject. Compare some of its passages with passages from another prose-poet, Oscar Wilde, where no veil of phantasy comes between the percipient and the thing perceived, and it will be strange if the reader does not feel that the later writer has a finer instinct for the choice and use of words.

It would be untrue to say that Wilde's instinct was faultless. A garish artificiality spoils much of his work; but this was through wilful perversity. Even in his earlier work—in that wonderful book, *Dorian Gray*, he realized the compelling charm of simplicity in style. His fairy stories, *The Happy Prince*, for instance, are little masterpieces of simple, restrained writing, and in the last things that came from his pen there is a growing appreciation of the value of simplicity.

De Quincey never realized this; he recognized one form of art—the decorative. And although he became a master of that form, it was inevitable that at times this mode of art should fail in its effect.

Here is a passage from *Levana and Our Ladies of Sorrow*:—

> "The eldest of the three is named Mater Lachrymarum, Our Lady of Tears. She it is that night and day raves and moans, calling for vanished faces. She stood in Rama, where a voice was heard of lamentation—Rachel weeping for her children, and refusing to be comforted. She it was that stood in Bethlehem on the night when Herod's sword swept its nurseries of Innocents, and the little feet were stiffened for ever which were heard at times as they trotted along floors overhead, woke pulses of love in household hearts that were not unmarked in heaven. Her eyes are sweet and subtle; wild and sleepy by turns; often times rising to the clouds, often times challenging the heavens. She wears a diadem round her head. And I knew by childish memories that she could go abroad upon the winds, when she heard the sobbing of litanies or the thundering of organs, and when she beheld the mustering of summer clouds."

And here is Oscar Wilde in *De Profundis*:—

> "Prosperity, pleasure, and success, may be rough of grain and common in fibre, but sorrow is the most sensitive of all created things. There is nothing that stirs in the whole world of thought to which sorrow does not vibrate in terrible and exquisite pulsation.... It is a wound that bleeds

when any hand but that of love touches it, and even then must bleed again, though not in pain. Behind joy and laughter there may be a temperament coarse, hard, and callous. But behind sorrow there is always sorrow. Pain, unlike pleasure, wears no mask. Truth in Art is . . . no echo coming from a hollow hill, any more than it is a silver well of water in the valley that shows the moon to the moon, and Narcissus to Narcissus. Truth in Art is the unity of a thing with itself—the soul made incarnate, the body instinct with spirit. For this reason there is no truth comparable to sorrow. There are times when sorrow seems to me to be the only truth. Other things may be illusions of the eye or the appetite made to blind the one and clog the other, but out of sorrow have the worlds been built, and at the birth of a child or a star there is pain."

I have not quoted these passages in order to pit one style against another; for each writer sets himself about a different task. A "dream fugue" demands a treatment other than the simpler, more direct treatment essential for Wilde's purpose. It is not because De Quincey the artist chose this especial form for once in order to portray a mood that the passage merits consideration; but because De Quincey always treated his emotional experiences as "dream fugues." Of suffering and privation, of pain and anguish bodily and mental, he had experiences more than the common lot. But when he tries to show this bleeding reality to us a mist invariably arises, and we see things "as in a glass darkly."

There is a certain passage in his Autobiography which affords a key to this characteristic of his work.

When quite a boy he had constituted himself imaginary king of an imaginary kingdom of Gombrom. Speaking of this fancy he writes: "O reader! do not laugh! I lived for ever under the terror of two separate wars and two separate worlds; one against the factory boys in a real world of flesh and blood, of stones and brickbats, of flight and pursuit, that were anything but figurative; the other in a world purely aerial, where all the combats and the sufferings were absolute moonshine. And yet the simple truth is that for anxiety and distress of mind the reality (which almost every morning's light brought round) was as nothing in comparison of that Dream Kingdom which rose like a vapour from my own brain, and which apparently by the fiat of my will could be for ever dissolved. Ah, but no! I had contracted obligations to Gombrom; I had submitted my conscience to a yoke; and in secret truth my will had no autocratic power. Long contemplation of a shadow, earnest study for the welfare of that shadow, sympathy with the wounded sensibilities of that shadow under accumulated wrongs; these bitter experiences, nursed by brooding thought, had gradually frozen that shadow into a region of reality far denser than the material realities of brass or granite."

This confession is a remarkable testimony to the reality of De Quincey's imaginative life. "I had contracted obligations to Gombrom." Yes, despite his practical experiences with the world, it was Gombrom, "the moonlight" side of things, that appealed to him. The boys might fling stones and brickbats, just as the world did later—but though he felt the onslaught, it moved him far less than did the phantasies of his imagination.

There is no necessity to weigh Wilde's experiences of "Our Ladies of Sorrow" beside those of De Quincey. All we need ask is which impresses us the more keenly with the actuality of sorrow. And I think there can be no doubt that it is not De Quincey.

"The Dream Kingdom that rose like a vapour" from his brain, this it was—this Vagabond imagination of his—that was the one great reality in life. It is a mistake to assume, as some have done, that this faculty for daydreaming was a legacy of the opium-eating. The opium gave an added brilliance to the dream-life, but it did not create it. He was a dreamer from his birth—a far more thorough-going dreamer than was ever Coleridge. There was a strain of insanity about him undoubtedly, and it says much for his intellectual activity and moral power that the Dream Kingdom did not disturb his mental life more than it did. Had he never touched opium to relieve his gastric complaint, he would have been eccentric—that is, if he had lived. Without some narcotic it is doubtful whether his highly sensitive organization would have survived the attacks of disease. As it was, the opium not only eased the pain, but lifted his imagination above the ugly realities of life, and afforded a solace in times of loneliness and misery.

III

Intellectually he was a man of a conservative turn of mind, with an ingrained respect for the conventions of life, but temperamentally he was a restless Vagabond, with a total disregard for the amenities of civilization, asking for nothing except to live out his own dream-life. Dealing with him as a writer, you found a shrewd, if wayward critic, with no little of "John Bull" in his composition. Deal with him as a man, you found a bright, kindly, nervous little man in a chronic state of shabbiness, eluding the attention of friends so far as possible, and wandering about town and country as if he had nothing in common with the rest of mankind. His Vagabondage is shown best in his purely imaginative work, and in the autobiographical sketches.

Small and insignificant in appearance to the casual observer, there was something arresting, fascinating about the man that touched even the irascible Carlyle. Much of his work, one can well understand, seemed to this lover of facts "full of wire-drawn ingenuities." But with all his contempt for phantasy, there was a touch of the dreamer in Carlyle, and the imaginative beauty, apart from the fanciful prettiness in De Quincey's work, would have appealed to him. For there was power, intellectual grip, behind the shifting fancies, and both as a critic and historian he has left behind him memorable work. As critic he has been taken severely to task for his judgments on French writers and on many lights of eighteenth-century thought. Certainly De Quincey's was not the type of mind we should go to for an interpretative criticism of the eighteenth century. Yet we must not forget his admirable appreciation of Goldsmith. At his best, as in his criticism of Milton and Wordsworth, he shows a fine, delicate, analytical power, which it is hard to overpraise.

"Obligations to Gombrom" do not afford the best qualification for the historian. One can imagine the hair rising in horror on the head of the late Professor Freeman at the idea of the opium-eater sitting down seriously to write history.

Yet he had, like Froude, the power of seizing upon the spectacular side of great movements which many a more accurate historian has lacked. Especially striking is his *Revolt of the Tartars*—the flight eastward of a Tartar nation across the vast steppes of Asia, from Russia to Chinese territory. Ideas impressed him rather than facts, and episodes rather than a continuous chain of events. But when he was interested, he had the power of describing with picturesque power certain dramatic episodes in a nation's history.

A characteristic of the literary Vagabond is the eager versatility of his intellectual interests. He will follow any path that promises to be interesting, not so much with the scholar's patient investigation as with the pedestrian's delight in "fresh woods and pastures new."

A prolific writer for the magazines, it is inevitable that there should be a measure that is ephemeral in De Quincey's voluminous writings. But it is impossible not to be struck by the wide range of his intellectual interests. A mind that is equally at home in the economics of Ricardo and the transcendentalism of Wordsworth; that can turn with undiminished zest from Malthus to Kant; that could deal lucidly with the "Logic of Political Economy," despite the dream-world that finds expression in the "impassioned prose"; that could delight in such broadly farcical absurdities as "*Sortilege and Astrology*," and such delicately suggestive studies as "On the Knocking at the Gate in Macbeth," a mind of this adventurous and varied type is assuredly a very remarkable one. That he should touch every subject with equal power was not to be expected, but the analytic brilliance that characterizes even his mystical writings enabled him to treat such subjects as political economy with a sureness of touch and a logical grasp that has astonished those who had regarded him as merely an inconsequential dreamer of dreams.

IV

I cannot agree with Dr. Japp [48] when, in the course of some laudatory remarks on De Quincey's humour, he says: "It is precisely here that De Quincey parts company, alike from Coleridge and from Wordsworth; neither of them had humour."

In the first place De Quincey's humour never seems to me very genuine. He could play with ideas occasionally in a queer fantastic way, as in his elaborate gibe on Dr. Andrew Bell.

> "First came Dr. Andrew Bell. We knew him. Was he dull? Is a wooden spoon dull? Fishy were his eyes, torpedinous was his manner; and his main idea, out of two which he really had, related to the moon—from which you infer, perhaps, that he was lunatic. By no means. It was no craze, under the influence of the moon, which possessed him; it was an idea of mere hostility to the moon. . . . His wrath did not pass into lunacy; it produced simple distraction; and uneasy fumbling with the idea—like that of an old superannuated dog who longs to worry, but cannot for want of teeth."

A clever piece of analytical satire, if you like, but not humorous so much as witty. Incongruity, unexpectedness, belongs to the essence of humour. Here there is that cunning display of congruity between the old dog and the Doctor which the wit is so adroit in evolving.

Similarly in the essay on "Murder considered as one of the Fine Arts," the style of clever extravaganza adopted in certain passages is witty, certainly, but lacks the airy irresponsibility characterizing humour. Sometimes he indulges in pure clowning, which is humorous in a heavy-handed way. But grimacing humour is surely a poor kind of humour.

Without going into any dismal academic discussion on Wit and Humour, I think it is quite possible to differentiate these two offsprings of imagination, making Wit the intellectual brother of the twain. Analytical minds naturally turn to wit, by preference: Impressionistic minds to humour. Dickens, who had no gift for analysis, and whose writings are a series of delightful unreflective, personal impressions, is always humorous, never witty. Reflective writers like George Eliot or George Meredith are more often witty than humorous.

I do not rate De Quincey's wit very highly, though it is agreeably diverting at times, but it was preferable to his humour.

The second point to be noted against Dr. Japp is his reference to Coleridge. No one would claim Wordsworth as a humorist, but Coleridge cannot be dismissed with this comfortable finality. Perhaps he was more witty than humorous; he also had an analytic mind of rarer quality even than De Quincey's, and his *Table Talk* is full of delightful flashes. But the amusing account he gives of his early journalistic experiences and the pleasant way in which he pokes fun at himself, can scarcely be compatible with the assertion that he had "no humour."

Indeed, it was this quality, I think, which endeared him especially to Lamb, and it was the absence of this quality which prevented Lamb from giving that personal attachment to Wordsworth which he held for both Coleridge and Hazlitt.

But the comparative absence of humour in De Quincey is another characteristic of Vagabondage. Humour is largely a product of civilization, and the Vagabond is only half-civilized. I can see little genuine humour in either Hazlitt or De Quincey. They had wit to an extent, it is true, but they had this despite, not because, of their Vagabondage. Thoreau, notwithstanding flashes of shrewd American wit, can scarcely be accounted a humorist. Whitman was entirely devoid of humour. A lack of humour is felt as a serious deficiency in reading the novels of Jefferies; and the airy wit of Stevenson is scarcely full-bodied enough to rank him among the humorists.

This deficiency of humour may be traced to the characteristic attitude of the Vagabond towards life, which is one of eager curiosity. He is inquisitive about its many issues, but with a good deal of the child's eagerness to know how a thing happened, and who this is, and what that is. Differing in many ways, as did Borrow and De Quincey, we find the same insatiable curiosity; true, it expressed itself differently, but there is a basic similarity between the impulse that took Borrow over the English highways and gave him that zest for travel in other countries, and the impulse that sent De Quincey wandering over the various roads of intellectual and emotional inquiry. Thoreau's main reason for his two years' sojourn in the woods was one of curiosity. He "wanted to know" what he could find out by "fronting" for a while the essential facts of life, and he left, as he says, "for as good a reason as I went there. Perhaps it seemed to me that I had several more lives to live." In other words, inquisitiveness inspired the experiment, and inquisitiveness as to other experiments induced him to terminate the Walden episode.

Now, in his own way, De Quincey was possibly the most inquisitive of all the Vagabonds. The complete absence of the imperative mood in his writings has moved certain moralists like Carlyle to impatience with him. There is a fine moral tone about his disposition, but his writings are engagingly unmoral (quite different, of course, from immoral). He has called himself "an intellectual creature," and this happy epithet exactly describes him. He collected facts, as an enthusiast collects curios, for purposes of decoration. He observed them, analysed their features, but almost always with a view to æsthetic comparisons.

And to understand De Quincey aright one must follow him in his multitudinous excursions, not merely rest content with a few fragments of "impassioned prose," and the avowedly autobiographic writings. For the autobiography extends through the sixteen volumes of his works. The writings, no doubt, vary in quality; in many, as in the criticism of German and French writers, acute discernment and astounding prejudices jostle one another. But this is no reason for turning impatiently away. Indeed, it is an additional incentive to proceed, for they supply such splendid psychological material for illustrating the temperament and tastes of the writer. And this may confidently be said: There is "fundamental brainwork" in every article that De Quincey has written.

V

What gives his works their especial attraction is not so much the analytic faculty, interesting as it is, or the mystical turn of mind, as in the piquant blend of the two. Thus, while he is poking fun at Astrology or Witchcraft, we are conscious all the time that he retains a sneaking fondness for the occult. He delights in dreams, omens, and coincidences. He reminds one at times of the lecturer on "Superstitions," who, in the midst of a brilliant analysis of its futility and absurdity, was interrupted by a black cat walking on to the platform, and was so disturbed by this portent that he brought his lecture to an abrupt conclusion.

On the whole the Mystic trampled over the Logician. His poetic imagination impresses his work with a rich inventiveness, while the logical faculty, though subsidiary, is utilized for giving form and substance to the visions.

It is curious to contrast the stateliness of De Quincey's literary style, the elaborate full-dress manner, with the extreme simplicity of the man. One might be tempted to add, surely here the style is *not* the man. His friends have testified that he was a gentle, timid, shrinking little man, and abnormally sensitive to giving offence; and to those whom he cared for—his family, for instance—he was the incarnation of affection and tenderness.

Yet in the writings we see another side, a considerable sprinkle of sturdy prejudices, no little self-assertion and pugnacity. But there is no real disparity. The style is the man here as ever. When roused by opposition he could even in converse show the claws beneath the velvet. Only the militant, the more aggressive side of the man is expressed more readily in his writings. And the gentle and amiable side more readily in personal intimacy. Both the life and the writings are wanted to supply a complete picture.

In one respect the records of his life efface a suspicion that haunts the reader of his works. More than once the reader is apt to speculate as to how far the arrogance that marks certain of his essays is a superficial quality, a literary trick; how far a moral trait. The record of his conversations tends to show that much of this was merely surface. Unlike Coleridge, unlike Carlyle, he was as willing to listen as to talk; and he said many of his best things with a delightful unconsciousness that they were especially good. He never seemed to have the least wish to impress people by his cleverness or aptness of speech.

But when all has been said as to the personality of the man as expressed in his writings—especially his *Confessions*, and to his personality as interpreted by friends and acquaintances—there remains a measure of mystery about De Quincey. This is part of his fascination, just as it is part of the fascination attaching to Coleridge. The frank confidences of his *Confessions* hide from view the inner ring of reserve, which gave a strange impenetrability to his character, even to those who knew and loved him best. A simple nature and a complex temperament.

Well, after all, such personalities are the most interesting of all, for each time we greet them it is with a note of interrogation.

III
GEORGE BORROW

"The common sun, the air, the skies,
To him are opening Paradise."

GRAY.

"He had an English look; that is was square
In make, of a complexion white and ruddy."

BYRON.

I

Why is it that almost as soon as we can toddle we eagerly demand a story of our elders? Why is it that the most excitable little girl, the most incorrigible little boy can be quieted by a teaspoonful of the jam of fiction? Why is it that "once upon a time" can achieve what moral strictures are powerless to effect?

It is because to most of us the world of imagination is the world that matters. We live in the "might be's" and "peradventures." Fate may have cast our lot in prosaic places; have predetermined our lives on humdrum lines; but it cannot touch our dreams. There we are princes, princesses—possessed of illimitable wealth, wielding immeasurable power. Our bodies may traverse the same dismal streets day after day; but our minds rove luxuriantly through all the kingdoms of the earth.

Those wonderful eastern stories of the "Flying Horse" and the "Magic Carpet," symbolize for us the matter-of-fact world and the matter-of-dream world. Nay, is there any sound distinction between facts and dreams? After all—

"We are such stuff
As dreams are made on, and our little life
Is rounded with a sleep."

But there are dreams and dreams—dreams by moonlight and dreams by sunlight. Literature can boast of many fascinating moonlight dreams—Ancient Mariners and Christabels, Wonder Books and Tanglewood Tales. And the fairies and goblins, the witches and wizards, were they not born by moonlight and nurtured under the glimmer of the stars?

But there are dreams by sunlight and visions at noonday also. Such dreams thrill us in another but no less unmistakable way, especially when the dreamer is a Scott, a William Morris, a Borrow.

And dreamers like Borrow are not content to see visions and dream dreams, their bodies must participate no less than their minds. They must needs set forth in quest of the unknown. Hardships and privations deter them not. Change, variety, the unexpected, these things are to them the very salt of life.

This untiring restlessness keeps a Richard Burton rambling over Eastern lands, turns a Borrow into the high-road and dingle. This bright-eyed Norfolk giant took more kindly to the roughnesses of life than did Hazlitt and De Quincey. Quite as neurotic in his way, his splendid physique makes us think of him as the embodiment of fine health. Illness and Borrow do not agree. We think of him swinging along the road like one of Dumas' lusty adventurers, exhibiting his powers of horsemanship, holding his own with well-seasoned drinkers—especially if the drink be Norfolk ale—conversing with any picturesque rag-tag and bob-tail he might happen upon. There is plenty of fresh air in his pages. No thinker like Hazlitt, no dreamer like De Quincey; but a shrewd observer with the most amazing knack of ingratiating himself with strangers.

No need for this romancer to seek distant lands for inspiration. Not even the villages of Spain and Portugal supplied him with such fine stuff for romance as Mumper's Dingle. He would get as strange a story out of a London counting-house or an old apple-woman on London Bridge as did many a teller of tales out of lonely heaths and stormy seas.

Lavengro and *The Romany Rye* are fine specimens of romantic autobiography. His life was varied enough, abounding in colour; but the Vagabond is never satisfied with things that merely happen. He is equally concerned with the things that might happen, with the things that ought to happen. And so Borrow added to his own personal record from the storehouse of dreams. Some have blamed him for not adhering to the actual facts. But does any autobiographer adhere to actual facts? Can any man, even with the most sensitive feeling for accuracy, confine himself to a record of what happened?

Of course not. The moment a man begins to write about himself, to delve in the past, to ransack the storehouse of his memory; then—if he has anything of the literary artist about him, and otherwise his book will not be worth the paper it is written on—he will take in a partner to assist him. That partner's name is Romance.

As a revelation of temperament, the *Confessions* of Rousseau and the *Mémoires* of Casanova are, one feels, delightfully trustworthy. But no sane reader ever imagines that he is reading an accurate transcript from the life of these adventurous gentlemen. The difference between the editions of De

Quincey's *Opium Eater* is sufficient to show how the dreams have expanded under popular approbation.

Borrow himself suggests this romantic method when he says, "What is an autobiography? Is it a mere record of a man's life, or is it a picture of the man himself?" Certainly, no one carried the romantic colouring further than he did. When he started to write his own life in *Lavengro* he had no notion of diverging from the strict line of fact. But the adventurer Vagabond moved uneasily in the guise of the chronicler. He wanted more elbow-room. He remembered all that he hoped to encounter, and from hopes it was no far cry to actualities.

Things might have happened so! Ye gods, they *did* happen so! And after all it matters little to us the exact proportion of fact and fiction. What does matter is that the superstructure he has raised upon the foundation of fact is as strange and unique as the palace of Aladdin.

However much he suggested the typical Anglo-Saxon in real life, there was the true Celt whenever he took pen in hand.

A stranger blend of the Celt and the Saxon indeed it would be hard to find. The Celtic side is not uppermost in his temperament—this strong, assertive, prize-fighting, beer-loving man (a good drinker, but never a

drunkard) seems far more Saxon than anything else. De Quincey had no small measure of the John Bull in his temperament, and Borrow had a great deal more. The John Bull side was very obvious. Yet a Celt he was by parentage, and the Celtic part was unmistakable, though below the surface. If the East Anglian in him had a weakness for athleticism, boiled mutton and caper sauce, the Celt in him responded quickly to the romantic associates of Wales.

Readers of Mr. Watts-Dunton's charming romance *Aylwin* will recall the emphasis laid on the passionate love of the Welsh for a tiny strip of Welsh soil. Borrow understood all this; he had a rare sympathy with the Cymric Celt. You can trace the Celt in his scenic descriptions, in his feeling for the spell of antiquity, his restlessness of spirit. And yet in his appearance there was little to suggest the Celt. Small wonder that many of his friends spoke of this white-haired giant of six foot three as if he was first and foremost an excellent athlete.

Certainly he had in full measure an Englishman's delight and proficiency in athletics—few better at running, jumping, wrestling, sparring, and swimming.

In many respects indeed Borrow will not have realized the fancy picture of the Englishman as limned by Hawthorne's fancy—the big, hearty, self-opiniated, beef-eating, ale-drinking John Bull. Save to a few intimates like Mr. Watts-Dunton and Dr. Hake he seems to have concealed very effectually the Celtic sympathies in his nature. But no reader of his books can be blind to this side of his character; and then again, as in all the literary Vagabonds, it is the complexity of the man's temperament that attracts and fascinates.

The man who can delight in the garrulous talk of a country inn, understand the magic of big solitudes; who can keenly appraise the points of a horse and feel the impalpable glamour of an old ruin; who will present an impenetrable reserve to the ordinary stranger and take the fierce, moody gypsy to his heart; who will break almost every convention of civilization, yet in the most unexpected way show a sturdy element of conventionality; a man, in short, of so many bewildering contradictions and strangely assorted qualities as Borrow cannot but compel interest.

Many of the contradictory traits were not, as they seemed, the inconsequential moods of an irresponsible nature, but may be traced to the fierce egotism of the man. The Vagabond is always an egotist; the egotism may be often amusing, and is rarely uninteresting. But the personal point of view, the personal impression, has for him the most tremendous importance. It makes its possessor abnormally sensitive to any circumstances, any environment, that may restrict his independence or prevent the full expression of his personal tastes and whims. Among our Vagabonds the two most pronounced egotists are Borrow and Whitman. The secret of their influence, their merits, and their deficiencies lies in this intense concentration of self. An appreciation of this quality leads us to comprehend a good deal of Borrow's attitude towards men and women. Reading *Lavengro* and *The Romany Rye* the reader is no less struck by the remarkable interest that Borrow takes in the people—especially the rough, uncultured people—whom he comes across, as in the cheerful indifference with which he loses sight of them and passes on to fresh characters. There is very little objective feeling in his friendships; as flesh and blood personages with individualities of their own—loves, hopes, faiths of their own—he seems to regard them scarcely at all. They exist chiefly as material for his curiosity and inquisitiveness. Hence there is a curious selfishness about him—not the selfishness of a passionate, capricious nature, but the selfishness of a self-absorbed and self-contained nature. Perhaps there was hidden away somewhere in his nature a strain of tenderness, of altruistic affection, which was reserved for a few chosen souls. But the warm human touch is markedly absent from his writings, despite their undeniable charm.

Take the Isopel Berners episode. Whether Isopel Berners was a fiction of the imagination or a character in real life matters not for my purpose. At any rate the episode, his friendship with this Anglo-Saxon girl of the road, is one of the distinctive features of both *Lavengro* and *The Romany Rye*. The attitude of Borrow towards her may safely be regarded as a clear indication of the man's character.

A girl of fine physical presence and many engaging qualities such as were bound to attract a man of Borrow's type, who had forsaken her friends to throw in her lot with this fellow-wanderer on the road. Here were the ready elements of a romance—of a friendship that should burn up with the consuming power of love the baser elements of self in the man's disposition, and transform his nature.

And what does he do?

He accepts her companionship, just as he might have accepted the companionship of one of his landlords or ostlers; spends the time he lived with her in the Dingle in teaching her Armenian, and when at last, driven to desperation by his calculating coldness, she comes to take farewell of him, he makes her a perfunctory offer of marriage, which she, being a girl of fine mettle as well as of strong affection, naturally declines. She leaves him, and after a few passages of philosophic regret, he passes on to the next adventure.

Now Borrow, as we know, was not physically drawn towards the ordinary gypsy type—the dark, beautiful Celtic women; and it was in girls of the fair Saxon order such as Isopel Berners that he sought a natural mate.

Certainly, if any woman was calculated by physique and by disposition to attract Borrow, Isopel Berners was that woman. And when we find that the utmost extent of his passion is to make tea for her and instruct her in Armenian, it is impossible not to be disagreeably impressed by the unnatural chilliness of such a disposition. Not even Isopel could break down the barrier of intense egoism that fenced him off from any profound intimacy with his fellow-creatures.

Perhaps Dr. Jessop's attack upon him errs in severity, and is to an extent, as Mr. Watts-Dunton says, "unjust"; but there is surely an element of truth in his remarks when he says: "Of anything like animal passion there is not a trace in all his many volumes. Not a hint that he ever kissed a woman or even took a little child upon his knee." Nor do I think that the anecdote which Mr. Watts-Dunton relates about the beautiful gypsy, to whom Borrow read Arnold's poem, goes far to dissipate the impression of Borrow's insensibility to a woman's charm.

A passing tribute to the looks of an extraordinarily beautiful girl is quite compatible with a comparative insensibility to feminine beauty and feminine graces. That Borrow was devoid of animal passion I do not believe—nor indeed do his books convey that impression; that he had no feeling for beauty either would be scarcely compatible with the Celtic element in his nature. I think it less a case—as Dr. Jessop seems to think—of want of passion as of a tyrannous egotism that excluded any element likely to prove troublesome. He would not admit a disturbing factor—such as the presence of the self-reliant Isopel—into his life.

No doubt he liked Isopel well enough in his fashion. Otherwise certainly he would not have made up his mind to marry her. But his own feelings, his own tastes, his own fancies, came first. He would marry her—oh yes!—there was plenty of time later on. For the present he could study her character, amuse himself with her idiosyncrasies, and as a return for her devotion and faithful affection teach her Armenian. Extremely touching!

But the episode of Isopel Berners is only one illustration, albeit a very significant one, of Borrow's calculating selfishness. No man could prove a more interesting companion than he; but one cannot help feeling that he was a sorry kind of friend.

It may seem strange at first sight, finding this wanderer of the road in the pay of the Bible Society, and a zealous servant in the cause of militant Protestantism. But the violent "anti-Popery" side of Borrow is only another instance of his love of independence. The brooding egotism that chafed at the least control was not likely to show any sympathy with sacerdotalism.

There was no trace of philosophy in Borrow's frankly expressed views on religious subjects. They were honest and straightforward enough, with all the vigorous unreflective narrowness of ultra-Protestantism.

It says much for the amazing charm of Borrow's writing that *The Bible in Spain* is very much better than a glorified tract. It must have come as a surprise to many a grave, pious reader of the Bible Society's publications.

And the Bible Society made the Vagabond from the literary point of view. Borrow's book—*The Zincali*—or an account of the gypsies of Spain, published in 1841, had brought his name before the public. But *The Bible in Spain* (1843) made him famous—doubtless to the relief of "glorious John Murray," the publisher, who was doubtful about the book's reception.

It is a fascinating book, and if lacking the unique flavour of the romantic autobiographies, *Lavengro* and *The Romany Rye*, has none the less many of the characteristics that give all his writings their distinctive attraction.

II

Can we analyse the charm that Borrow's books and Borrow's personality exercise over us, despite the presence of unpleasing traits which repel?

In the first place he had the faculty for seizing upon the picturesque and picaresque elements in the world about him. He had the ready instinct of the discursive writer for what was dramatically telling. Present his characters in dramatic form he could not; one and all pass through the crucible of his temperament before we see them. We feel that they are genuinely observed, but they are Borrovized. They speak the language of Borrow. While this is quite true, it is equally true that he knows exactly how to impress and interest the reader with the personages.

Take this effective little introduction to one of the characters in *The Bible in Spain*:—

> "At length the moon shone out faintly, when suddenly by its beams I beheld a figure moving before me at a slight distance. I quickened the pace of the burra, and was soon close at its side. It went on, neither altering its pace nor looking round for a moment. It was the figure of a man, the tallest and bulkiest that I had hitherto seen in Spain, dressed in a manner strange and singular for the country. On his head was a hat with a low crown and broad brim, very much resembling that of an English waggoner; about his body was a long loose tunic or slop, seemingly of coarse ticken, open in front, so as to allow the interior garments to be occasionally seen; these appeared to consist of a jerkin and short velveteen pantaloons. I have said that the brim of the hat was broad, but broad as it was, it was insufficient to cover an immense bush of coal-black hair, which, thick and curly, projected on either side; over the left shoulder was flung a kind of satchel, and in the right hand was held a long staff or pole.

"There was something peculiarly strange about the figure, but what struck me the most was the tranquillity with which it moved along, taking no heed of me, though, of course, aware of my proximity, but looking straight forward along the road, save when it occasionally raised a huge face and large eyes towards the moon, which was now shining forth in the eastern quarter.

"'A cold night,' said I at last. 'Is this the way to Talavera?'

"'It is the way to Talavera, and the night is cold.'

"'I am going to Talavera,' said I, 'as I suppose you are yourself.'

"'I am going thither, so are you, *Bueno.*'

"The tones of the voice which delivered these words were in their way quite as strange and singular as the figure to which the voice belonged; they were not exactly the tones of a Spanish voice, and yet there was something in them that could hardly be foreign; the pronunciation also was correct, and the language, though singular, faultless. But I was most struck with the manner in which the last word, *bueno*, was spoken. I had heard something like it before, but where or when I could by no means remember. A pause now ensued; the figure stalking on as before with the most perfect indifference, and seemingly with no disposition either to seek or avoid conversation.

"'Are you not afraid,' said I at last, 'to travel these roads in the dark? It is said that there are robbers abroad.'

"'Are you not rather afraid,' replied the figure, 'to travel these roads in the dark—you who are ignorant of the country, who are a foreigner, an Englishman!'

"'How is it that you know me to be an Englishman?' demanded I, much surprised.

"'That is no difficult matter,' replied the figure; 'the sound of your voice was enough to tell me that.'

"'You speak of voices,' said I; 'suppose the tone of your own voice were to tell me who you are?'

"'That it will not do,' replied my companion; 'you know nothing about me—you can know nothing about me.'

"'Be not sure of that, my friend; I am acquainted with many things of which you have little idea.'

"'Por exemplo,' said the figure.

"'For example,' said I, 'you speak two languages.'

"The figure moved on, seemed to consider a moment, and then said slowly, '*Bueno.*'

"'You have two names,' I continued; 'one for the house and the other for the street; both are good, but the one by which you are called at home is the one which you like best.'

"The man walked on about ten paces, in the same manner as he had previously done; all of a sudden he turned, and taking the bridle of the burra gently in his hand, stopped her. I had now a full view of his face and figure, and those huge features and Herculean form still occasionally revisit me in my dreams. I see him standing in the moonshine, staring me in the face with his deep calm eyes. At last he said—

"'Are you then one of us?'"

An admirable sketch, adroitly conceived and executed beyond doubt, but as a fragment of dialogue remarkable for its literary skill rather than for its characterization.

His instinct for the picturesque never fails him. This is one of the reasons why, despite his astounding garrulousness, the readers of his books are never wearied.

Whether it be a ride in the forest, a tramp on foot, an interview with some individual who has interested him, the picturesque side is always presented, and never is he at better advantage than when depicting some scene of gypsy life.

Opening *The Bible in Spain* at random I happen on this description of a gypsy supper. It is certainly not one of the best or most picturesque, but as an average sample of his scenic skill it will serve its purpose well.

"Hour succeeded hour, and still we sat crouching over the brasero, from which, by this time, all warmth had departed; the glow had long since disappeared, and only a few dying sparks were to be distinguished. The room or hall was now involved in utter darkness; the women were motionless and still; I shivered and began to feel uneasy. 'Will Antonio be here to-night?' at length I demanded.

"'*No tenga usted cuidao*, my London Caloro,' said the gypsy mother, in an unearthly tone; 'Pepindorio [70] has been here some time.'

"I was about to rise from my seat and attempt to escape from the house, when I felt a hand laid upon my shoulder, and in a moment I heard the voice of Antonio.

"'Be not afraid, 'tis I, brother; we will have a light anon, and then supper.'

"The supper was rude enough, consisting of bread, cheese, and olive. Antonio, however, produced a leathern bottle of excellent wine; we dispatched these viands by the light of an earthern lamp which was placed upon the floor.

"'Now,' said Antonio to the youngest female, 'bring me the pajandi, and I will sing a gachapla.'

"The girl brought the guitar, which with some difficulty the gypsy tuned, and then, strumming it vigorously, he sang—

"I stole a plump and bonny fowl,
  But ere I well had dined,
The master came with scowl and growl,
  And me would captive bind.

"My hat and mantle off I threw,
  And scour'd across the lea,
Then cried the beng [71] with loud halloo,
  Where does the Gypsy flee?"

"He continued playing and singing for a considerable time, the two younger females dancing in the meanwhile with unwearied diligence, whilst the aged mother occasionally snapped her fingers or beat time on the ground with her stock. At last Antonio suddenly laid down the instrument.

"'I see the London Caloro is weary. Enough, enough; to-morrow more thereof—we will now to the *charipé* (bed).

"'With all my heart,' said I; 'where are we to sleep?'

"'In the stable,' said he, 'in the manger; however cold the stable may be, we shall be warm enough in the bufa.'"

Perhaps his power in this direction is more fully appreciated when he deals with material that promises no such wealth of colour as do gypsy scenes and wanderings in the romantic South.

Cheapside and London Bridge suit him fully as well as do Spanish forests or Welsh mountains. True romancer as he is, he is not dependent on conventionally picturesque externals for arresting attention; since he will discover the stuff of adventure wherever his steps may lead him. The streets of Bagdad in the "golden prime" of Haroun Alraschid are no more mysterious, more enthralling, than the well-known thoroughfares of modern London. No ancient sorceress of Eastern story can touch his imagination more deeply than can an old gypsy woman. A skirmish with a publisher is fully as exciting as a tilt in a medieval tourney; while the stories told him by a rural landlord promise as much relish as any of the tales recounted by Oriental barbers and one-eyed Calenders.

Thus it is that while the pervasive egotism of the man bewitches us, we yield readily to the spell of his splendid garrulity. It is of no great moment that he should take an occasional drink to quench his thirst when passing along the London streets. But he will continue to make even these little details interesting. Did he think fit to recount a sneeze, or to discourse upon the occasion on which he brushed his hair, he would none the less, I think, have held the reader's attention.

Here is the episode of a chance drink; it is a drink and nothing more; but it is not meant to be skipped, and does not deserve to be overlooked.

> "Notwithstanding the excellence of the London pavement, I began, about nine o'clock, to feel myself thoroughly tired; painfully and slowly did I drag my feet along. I also felt very much in want of some refreshment, and I remembered that since breakfast I had taken nothing. I was in the Strand, and glancing about I perceived that I was close by an hotel which bore over the door the somewhat remarkable name of 'Holy Lands.' Without a moment's hesitation I entered a well-lighted passage, and turning to the left I found myself in a well-lighted coffee-room, with a well-dressed and frizzled waiter before me. 'Bring me some claret,' said I, for I was rather faint than hungry, and I felt ashamed to give a humble order to so well-dressed an individual. The waiter looked at me for a moment, then making a low bow he bustled off, and I sat myself down in the box nearest to the window. Presently the waiter returned, bearing beneath his left arm a long bottle, and between the fingers of his right hand two purple glasses; placing the latter on the table, set the bottle down before me with a bang, and then standing still appeared to watch my movements. You think I don't know how to drink a glass of claret, thought I to myself. I'll soon show you how we drink claret where I come from; and

filling one of the glasses to the brim, I flickered it for a moment between my eyes and the lustre, and then held it to my nose; having given that organ full time to test the bouquet of the wine, I applied the glass to my lips. Taking a large mouthful of the wine, which I swallowed slowly and by degrees that the palate might likewise have an opportunity of performing its functions. A second mouthful I disposed of more summarily; then placing the empty glass upon the table, I fixed my eyes upon the bottle and said nothing; whereupon the waiter who had been observing the whole process with considerable attention, made me a bow yet more low than before, and turning on his heel retired with a smart chuck of the head, as much as to say, 'It is all right; the young man is used to claret.'"

A slight enough incident, but, like every line which Borrow wrote, intensely temperamental. How characteristic this of the man's attitude: "You think I don't know how to drink a glass of claret, thought I to myself." Then with what deliberate pleasure does he record the theatrical posing for the benefit of the waiter. How he loves to impress! You are conscious of this in every scene which he describes, and it is quite useless to resent it. The only way to escape it is by leaving Borrow unread. And this no wise man can do willingly.

The insatiable thirst for adventure, the passion for the picturesque and dramatic, were so constant with him, that it need not surprise us when he seizes upon every opportunity for mystifying and exciting interest. It is possible that the "veiled period" in his life about which he hints is veiled because it was a time of privation and suffering, and he is consequently anxious to forget it. But I do not think it likely. Nor do the remarks of Mr. Watts-Dunton on this subject support this theory. Indeed, Mr. Watts-Dunton, who knew him so intimately, and had ample occasion to note his love of "making a mystery," hints pretty plainly that "the veiled period" may well be a pleasant myth invented by Borrow just for the excitement of it, not because there was anything special to conceal, or because he wished to regard certain chapters in his life as a closed book.

III

Mention has been made of Borrow's feeling for the picaresque elements in life. Give him a rogue, a wastrel, any character with a touch of the untamed about him, and no one delighted him more in exhibiting the fascinating points of this character and his own power in attracting these rough, unsocial fellows towards him and eliciting their confidences. Failing the genuine article, however, Borrow had quite as remarkable a knack of giving even for conventional people and highly respectable thoroughfares a roguish and adventurous air. Indeed it was this sympathy with the picaresque side of life, this thorough understanding of the gypsy temperament, that gives Borrow's genius its unique distinction. Other characteristics, though important, are subsidiary to this. Writers such as Stevenson have given us discursive books of travel; other Vagabonds have shown an equal zest for the life of the open air—Thoreau and Whitman, for example. But contact with the gypsies revealed Borrow to himself, made him aware of his powers. It is not so much a case of like seeking like, as of like seeking unlike. Affinities there were, no doubt, between the Romany and the "Gorgio" Borrow, but they are strong temperamental differences. On the one side an easy, unconscious nonchalance, a natural vivacity; on the other a morbid self-consciousness and a pronounced strain of melancholy. And it was doubtless the contrast that appealed to him so strongly and helped him to throw off his habitual moody reserve.

For beneath that unpromising reserve, as a few chosen friends knew, and as the gypsies knew, there was a frank camaraderie that won their hearts.

Was he, one naturally asks, when once this barrier of reserve had been broken down, a lovable man? Certainly he seems to have won the affection of the gypsies; and the warm admiration of men like Mr. Watts-Dunton points to an affirmative answer. And yet one hesitates. He attracted people, that cannot be gainsaid; he won many affections, that also is uncontrovertible. But to call a man lovable it is not sufficient that he should win affection, he must retain it. Was Borrow able to do this? There is the famous case of Isopel to answer in the negative. She loved him, but she found him out. Was it not so? How else explain the gradual change of demeanour, and the sad, disillusioned departure. Perhaps at first the independence of the man, his freedom from sentimentality, piqued, interested, and attracted her. This is often the case with women. They may fall in love with an unsentimental man, but they can never be happy with him.

Isopel retained a regard for her fellow-comrade of the road, but she would not be his wife.

Of his literary friends no one has written so warmly in defence of Borrow, or shown a more discerning admiration of his qualities than Mr. Watts-Dunton.

And yet in the warm tribute which Mr. Watts-Dunton has paid to Borrow I cannot help feeling that some of the illustrations he gives in justification of his eulogy are scarcely adequate. It may well be that he has a wealth of personal reminiscences which he could quote if so inclined, and make good his asseverations. As it is, one can judge only by what he tells us. And what does he tell us?

To show that Borrow took an interest in children, Mr. Watts-Dunton quotes a story about Borrow and the gipsy child which "Borrow was fond of telling in support of his anti-tobacco bias." The point of the story lies in the endeavours of Borrow to dissuade a gypsy woman from smoking her pipe, whilst his friend pointed out to the woman how the smoke was injuring the child whom she was suckling. Borrow used his friend's argument, which obviously appealed to the maternal instinct in order to persuade the woman to give up her pipe. There is no reason to think that Borrow was especially concerned for the child's welfare. What concerned him was a human being poisoning herself with nicotine, and his dislike particularly to see a woman smoking. After the woman had gone he said to his friend: "It ought to be a criminal offence for a woman to smoke at all." And that it was frankly as an anti-tobacco crusader that he considered the episode, is proved surely by Mr. Watts-Dunton himself, when he adds: "Whenever he (Borrow) was told, as he sometimes was, that what brought on the 'horrors' when he lived alone in the Dingle, was the want of tobacco, this story was certain to come up."

One cannot accept this as a specially striking instance of Borrow's interest in children, any more than the passing reference (already noted) to the extraordinarily beautiful gypsy girl, as an instance of his susceptibility to feminine charms.

Failing better illustrations at first hand, one turns toward his books, where he reveals so many characteristics, and here one is struck by the want of susceptibility, the obvious lack of interest in the other sex, showed by his few references to women, and what is even more significant the absence of any love story in his own life, apart from his books (his marriage with the well-to-do widow, though a happy one, can scarcely be called romantic). These things certainly outweigh the trivial incident which Mr. Watts-Dunton recalls.

As for the pipe episode, it reminds me of Macaulay's well-known gibe at the Puritans, who objected to bear-baiting, he says, less because it gave pain to the bear than because it gave pleasure to the spectators. Similarly his objection to the pipe seems not so much on account of the child suffering, as because the woman took pleasure in this "pernicious habit."

But enough of fault-finding. After all, Mr. Watts-Dunton has done a signal service to literature by preferring the claims of Borrow, and has upheld him loyally against attacks which were too frequently mean-spirited and unfair.

Obviously, Borrow was a man of an ingratiating personality, which is a very different thing from saying that he was a man with an ingratiating manner. Of all manners, the ingratiating is the one most likely to arouse suspicion in the minds of all but the most obtuse. An ingratiating personality, however, is one that without effort and in the simplest way attracts others, as a magnet attracts iron. Once get Borrow interested in a man, it followed quite naturally that the man was interested in Borrow. He might be a rough, unsociable fellow with whom others found it hard to get on, but Borrow would win his confidence in a few moments.

Borrow seemed to know exactly how to approach people, what to say, and how to say it. Sometimes he may have preferred to stand aloof in moody reserve; that is another matter. But given the inclination, he had a genius for companionship, as some men have a genius for friendship. As a rule it will be found that the Vagabond, the Wanderer, is far better as a companion than as friend. What he cares for is to smile, chatter, and pass on. Loyal he may be to those who have done him service, but he is not ready to encroach upon his own comfort and convenience for any man. Borrow remained steadfast to his friends, but a personal slight, even if not intended, he regarded as unforgivable.

The late Dr. Martineau was at school with him at Norwich, and after a youthful escapade on Borrow's part, Martineau was selected by the master as the boy to "horse" Borrow while he was undergoing corporal punishment. Probably the proceeding was quite as distasteful to the young Martineau as to the scapegrace. But Borrow never forgot the incident nor forgave the compulsory participator in his degradation. And years afterwards he declined to attend a social function when he had ascertained that Martineau would be there, making a point of deliberately avoiding him. Another instance this of the morbid egotism of the man.

Where, however, no whim or caprice stood in the way, Borrow reminds one of the man who knows as soon as he has tapped the earth with the "divining rod" whether or no there is water there. Directly he saw a man he could tell by instinct whether there was stuff of interest there; and he knew how to elicit it. And never is he more successful than when dealing with the "powerful, uneducated man." Consequently, no portion of his writings are more fascinating than when he has to deal with such figures. Who can forget his delightful pictures of the gypsy—"Mr. Petulengro"? Especially the famous meeting in *Lavengro*, when he and the narrator discourse on death.

> "'Life is sweet, brother.'
>
> "'Do you think so?'
>
> "'Think so! There's night and day, brother, both sweet things; sun, moon, and stars, brother, all sweet things; there's likewise a wind on the heath. Life is very sweet, brother. Who would wish to die?'
>
> "'I would wish to die.'

"'You talk like a Gorgio—which is the same as talking like a fool—were you a Romany chal you would talk wiser. Wish to die indeed! A Romany chal would wish to live for ever.'

"'In sickness, Jasper?'

"'There's the sun and stars, brother.'

"'In blindness, Jasper?'

"'There's the wind on the heath, brother; if I could only feel that, I would gladly live for ever. Dosta, we'll now go to the tents and put on the gloves; and I'll try to make you feel what a sweet thing it is to be alive.'"

Then again there is the inimitable ostler in *The Romany Rye*, whose talk exhales what Borrow would call "the wholesome smell of the stable." His wonderful harangues (Borrovized to a less extent than usual) have all the fine, breathless garrulity of this breed of man, and his unique discourse on "how to manage a horse on a journey" occupies a delightful chapter. Here are the opening sentences:—

"'When you are a gentleman,' said he, 'should you ever wish to take a journey on a horse of your own, and you could not have a much better than the one you have here eating its fill in the box yonder—I wonder, by the by, how you ever came by it—you can't do better than follow the advice I am about to give you, both with respect to your animal and yourself. Before you start, merely give your horse a couple of handfuls of corn and a little water, somewhat under a quart, and if you drink a pint of water yourself out of the pail, you will feel all the better during the whole day; then you may walk and trot your animal for about ten miles, till you come to some nice inn, where you may get down, and see your horse led into a nice stall, telling him not to feed him till you come. If the ostler happens to be a dog-fancier, and has an English terrier dog like that of mine there, say what a nice dog it is, and praise its black and fawn; and if he does not happen to be a dog-fancier, ask him how he's getting on, and whether he ever knew worse times; that kind of thing will please the ostler, and he will let you do just what you please with your own horse, and when your back is turned he'll say to his comrades what a nice gentleman you are, and how he thinks he has seen you before; then go and sit down to breakfast, get up and go and give your horse a feed of corn; chat with the ostler two or three minutes till your horse has taken the shine out of his oats, which will prevent the ostler taking any of it away when your back is turned, for such things are sometimes done—not that I ever did such a thing myself when I was at the inn at Hounslow; oh, dear me, no! Then go and finish your breakfast.'"

IV

It is interesting to compare Borrow's studies in unvarnished human nature with the characterizations of novelists like Mr. Thomas Hardy. Both Borrow and Hardy are drawn especially to rough primal characters, characters not "screened by conventions." As Mr. Hardy puts it in an essay contributed to the *Forum* in 1888.

> "The conduct of the upper classes is screened by conventions, and thus the real character is not easily seen; if it is seen it must be pourtrayed subjectively, whereas in the lower walks conduct is a direct expression of the inner life, and their characters can be directly pourtrayed through the act."

Mr. Hardy's rustics differ from Borrow's rustics, however, in the method of presentment. Mr. Hardy is always the sympathetic, amused observer. The reader of that delicious pastoral "Under the Greenwood Tree" feels that he is listening to a man who is recounting something he has overheard. The account is finely sympathetic, but there is an unmistakable note of philosophic detachment. The story-teller has enjoyed his company, but is obviously not of them. That is why he will gossip to you with such relish of humour. Borrow, on the other hand, speaks as one of them. He is far less amused by his garrulous ostlers and whimsical landlords than profoundly interested in them. Then again, though the Vagabond type appeals to Mr. Hardy, it appeals to him not because of any temperamental affinity, but because he happens to be a curious, wistful spectator of human life. He sees in the restless Vagabond an extreme example of the capricious sport of fate, but while his heart goes out to him his mind stands aloof.

Looking at their characterization from the literary point of view, it is evident that Mr. Hardy is the greater realist. He would give you *an* ostler, whereas Borrow gives you *the* ostler. Borrow knows his man thoroughly, but he will not trouble about little touches of individualization. We see the ostler vividly—we do not see the man—save on the ostler side. With Hardy we should see other aspects beside the ostler aspect of the man.

A novelist with whom Borrow has greater affinity is Charles Reade. There is the same quick, observant, unphilosophical spirit; the same preference for plain, simple folk, the same love of health and virility. And in *The Cloister and the Hearth*, one of the great romances of the world, one feels touches of the same Vagabond spirit as animates *Lavengro* and *The Romany Rye*. The incomparable Denys, with his favourite cry, "Le diable est mort," is a splendid study in genial vagrancy.

Literary comparisons, though they discover affinities, but serve to emphasize in the long run the distinctive originality of Borrow's writings.

He has himself admitted to the influence of Defoe and Lesage. But though his manner recalls at times the manner of Defoe, and though the form of his narrative reminds the reader of the Spanish rogue story, the psychological atmosphere is vastly different. He may have taken Defoe as his model just as Thackeray took Fielding; but *Vanity Fair* is not more unlike *Tom Jones* than is *Lavengro* unlike *Robinson Crusoe*.

It is idle to seek for the literary parentage of this Vagabond. Better far to accept him as he is, a wanderer, a rover, a curious taster of life, at once a mystic and a realist. He may have qualities that repel; but so full is he of contradictions that no sooner has the frown settled on the brow than it gives place to a smile. We may not always like him; never can we ignore him. Provocative, unsatisfying, fascinating—such is George Borrow. And most fascinating of all is his love of night, day, sun, moon, and stars, "all sweet things." Cribbed in the close and dusty purlieus of the city, wearied by the mechanical monotony of the latest fashionable novel, we respond gladly to the spacious freshness of *Lavengro* and *The Romany Rye*. Herein lies the spell of Borrow; for in his company there is always "a wind on the heath."

IV
HENRY D. THOREAU

"Enter these enchanted woods
You who dare."

GEORGE MEREDITH.

I

Thoreau has suffered badly at the hands of the critics. By some he has been regarded as a poser, and the Walden episode has been spoken of as a mere theatrical trick. By others he has been derided as a cold-blooded hermit, who fled from civilization and the intercourse of his fellows. Even Mr. Watts-Dunton, the eloquent friend of the Children of the Open Air, quite recently in his introduction to an edition of *Walden* has impugned his sincerity, and leaves the impression that Thoreau was an uncomfortable kind of egotist. He has not lacked friends, but his friends have not always written discreetly about him, thus giving the enemy opportunity to blaspheme. And while not unmindful of Mr. H. S. Salt's sympathetic biography, nor the admirable monograph by Mr. "H. A. Page," there is no denying the fact that the trend of modern criticism has been against him. The sarcastic comments of J. R. Lowell, and the banter of R. L. Stevenson, however we may disagree with them, are not to be lightly ignored, coming from critics usually so sane and discerning.

Since it is the Walden episode, the two years' sojourn in the woods near Concord, that has provoked the scornful ire of the critics, it may be well to re-examine that incident.

From his earliest years Thoreau was a lover of the open air. It was not merely a poetic appreciation such as Emerson had of the beauties of nature—though a genuine poetic imagination coloured all that he wrote—but an intellectual enthusiasm for the wonders of the natural world, and, most important of all, a deep and tender sympathy with all created things characteristic of the Eastern rather than the Western mind. He observed as a naturalist, admired like a poet, loved with the fervour of a Buddhist; every faculty of his nature did homage to the Earth.

Most of us will admit to a sentimental regard for the open air and for country sights and sounds. But in many cases it reduces itself to a vague liking for "pretty scenery" and an annual conviction that a change of air will do us good. And so it is that the man who prefers to live the greater part of his life in the open is looked upon either as a crank or a poser. Borrow's taste for adventure, and the picturesque vigour of his personality, help largely in our minds to condone his wandering instinct. But the more passive temperament of Thoreau, and the absence in his writings of any stuff of romance, lead us to feel a kind of puzzled contempt for the man.

"He shirks his duty as a citizen," says the practical Englishman; "He experienced nothing worth mentioning," says the lover of adventure. Certainly he lacked many of the qualities that make the literary Vagabond attractive—and for this reason many will deny him the right to a place among them—but he was neither a skulker nor a hermit.

In 1839, soon after leaving college, he made his first long jaunt in company with his brother John. This was a voyage on the Concord and Merrimac rivers—a pleasant piece of idling turned to excellent literary account. The volume dealing with it—his first book—gives sufficient illustration of his practical powers to dissipate the absurd notion that he was a mere sentimentalist. No literary Vagabond was ever more skilful with his hands than Thoreau. There was scarcely anything he could not do, from making lead pencils to constructing a boat. And throughout his life he supported himself by manual labour whenever occasion demanded. Had he been so disposed he could doubtless have made a fortune—for he had all the nimble versatility of the American character, and much of its shrewdness. His attacks, therefore, upon money-making, and upon the evils of civilization, are no mere vapourings of an incompetent, but the honest conviction of a man who believes he has chosen the better part.

In his *Walk to Wachusett* there are touches of genial friendliness with the simple, sincere country folk, and evidence that he was heartily welcome by them. Such a welcome would not have been vouchsafed to a cold-blooded recluse.

The keen enjoyment afforded to mind and body by these outings suggested to Thoreau the desirability of a longer and more intimate association with Nature. Walden Wood had been a familiar and favoured spot for many years, and so he began the building of his tabernacle there. So far from being a sudden, sensational resolve with an eye to effect, it was the natural outcome of his passion for the open.

He had his living to earn, and would go down into Concord from time to time to sell the results of his handiwork. He was quite willing to see friends and any chance travellers who visited from other motives than mere inquisitiveness. On the other hand, the life he proposed for himself as a temporary experiment would afford many hours of congenial solitude, when he could study the ways of the animals that he loved and give free expression to his naturalistic enthusiasms.

Far too much has been made of the Walden episode. It has been written upon as if it had represented the totality of Thoreau's life, instead of being merely an interesting episode. Critics have animadverted upon it, as if the time had been spent in brooding, self-pity, and sentimental affectations, as if Thoreau had gone there to escape from his fellow-men. All this seems to me wide of the mark. Thoreau was always keenly interested in men and manners; his essays abound in a practical sagacity, too frequently overlooked. He went to Walden not to escape from ordinary life, but to fit himself for ordinary life. The sylvan solitudes, as he knew, had their lessons for him no less than the busy haunts of men.

Of course it would be idle to deny that he found his greatest happiness in the woods and fields; it is this touch of wildness that makes of him a Vagabond. But though not an emotional man, his was not a hard nature so much as a reserved, self-centred nature, rarely expressing itself in outward show of feeling. That he was a man capable of strong affection is shown by his devotion to his brother. Peculiarities of temperament he had certainly, idiosyncrasies as marked as those of Borrow. These I wish to discuss later. For the moment I am concerned to defend him from the criticism that he was a loveless, brooding kind of creature, more interested in birds and fishes than in his fellow-men. For he was neither loveless nor brooding, and the characteristics that have proved most puzzling arose from the mingled strain in his nature of the Eastern quietist and the shrewd Western. These may now be considered more leisurely. I will deal with the less important first of all.

II

Some of his earlier work suffers somewhat from a too faithful discipleship of Emerson; but when he had found himself, as he has in *Walden*, he can break away from this tendency, and there are many lovely passages untouched by didacticism.

> "The stillness was intense and almost conscious, as if it were a natural sabbath. The air was so elastic and crystalline that it had the same effect on the landscape that a glass has on a picture—to give it an ideal remoteness and perfection. The landscape was bathed in a mild and quiet light, while the woods and fences chequered and partitioned it with new regularity, and rough and uneven fields stretched far away with lawnlike smoothness to the horizon, and the clouds, finely distinct and picturesque, seemed a fit drapery to hang over fairyland."

But while there is the Wordsworthian appreciation of the peaceful moods of Nature and of the gracious stillnesses, there is the true spirit of the Vagabond in his Earth-worship. Witness his pleasant "Essay on Walking":—

> "We are but faint-hearted crusaders; even the walkers nowadays undertake no persevering world's end enterprises. Our expeditions are but tours, and come round again at evening to the old hearthside from which we set out. Half of the walk is but retracing our steps. We should go forth on the shortest walks, perchance, in the spirit of stirring adventure, never to return, prepared to send back our embalmed hearts only as relics to our desolate kingdom. If you have paid your debts and made your will and settled all your affairs, and are a free man, then you are ready for a walk."

There is a relish in this sprightly abjuration that is transmittible to all but the dullest mind. The essay can take its place beside Hazlitt's "On Going a Journey," than which we can give it no higher praise.

With all his appreciation of the quieter, the gentler aspects of nature, he has the true hardiness of the child of the road, and has as cheery a welcome for the east wind as he has for the gentlest of summer breezes. Here is a little winter's sketch:—

> "The wonderful purity of Nature at this season is a most pleasing fact. Every decayed stump and moss-grown stone and rush of the dead leaves of autumn are concealed by a clean napkin of snow. In the bare fields and trickling woods see what virtue survives. In the coldest and bleakest places the warmest charities still maintain a foothold. A cold and searching wind drives away all contagion, and nothing can withstand it but what has a virtue in it; and accordingly whatever we meet with in cold and bleak places as the tops of mountains, we respect for a sort of sturdy innocence, a Puritan toughness."

But Thoreau's pleasant gossips about the woods in Maine, or on the Concord River, would pall after a time were they not interspersed with larger utterances and with suggestive illustrations from the Books of the East. Merely considered as "poet-naturalist" he cannot rank with Gilbert White for quaint simplicity, nor have his discursive essays the full, rich note that we find in Richard Jefferies. That his writings show a sensitive imagination as well as a quick observation the above extracts will show. But unfortunately he had contracted a bad attack of Emersonitis, from which as literary writer he never completely recovered. Salutary as Emerson was to Thoreau as an intellectual irritant, he was the last man in the world for the discursive Thoreau to take as a literary model.

Many fine passages in his writings are spoiled by vocal imitations of the "voice oracular," which is the more annoying inasmuch as Thoreau was no weak replica of Emerson intellectually, showing in some respects indeed a firmer grasp of the realities of life. But for some reason or other he grew enamoured of certain Emersonian mannerisms, which he used whenever he felt inclined to fire off a platitude. Sometimes he does it so well that it is hard to distinguish the disciple from his master. Thus:—

> "How can we expect a harvest of thought who have not a seedtime of character?"

Again:—

> "Only he can be trusted with goods who can present a face of bronze to expectations."

Unimpeachable in sentiment, but too obviously inspired for us to view them with satisfaction. And Thoreau at his best is so fresh, so original, that we decline to be put off with literary imitations, however excellently done.

And thus it is that Thoreau has been too often regarded as a mere disciple of Emerson. For this he cannot altogether escape blame, but the student will soon detect the superficiality of the criticism, and see the genuine Thoreau beneath the Emersonian veneer.

Thoreau lacked the integrating genius of Emerson, on the one hand, yet possessed an eye for concrete facts which the master certainly lacked. His strength, therefore, lay in another direction, and where Thoreau is seen at his best is where he is dealing with the concrete experiences of life, illustrating them from his wide and discursive knowledge of Indian character and Oriental modes of thought.

III

Insufficient attention has been paid, I think, to Thoreau's sympathy with the Indian character and his knowledge of their ways.

The Indians were to Thoreau what the gypsies were to Borrow. Appealing to certain spiritual affinities in the men's natures, they revealed their own temperaments to them, enabling them to see the distinctiveness of their powers. Thoreau was never quite able to give this intimate knowledge such happy literary expression as Borrow. Apprehending the peculiar charm, the power and limitations of the Indian character, appreciating its philosophical value, he lacked the picturesque pen of Borrow to visualize this for the reader.

A lover of Indian relics from his childhood, he followed the Indians into their haunts, and conversed with them frequently. Some of the most interesting passages he has written detail conversations with them. One feels he knew and understood them; and they no less understood him, and talked with him as they certainly would not have done with any other white man. But one would have liked to have heard much more about them. If only Thoreau could have given us an Indian Petulengro, how interesting it would have been!

But, like the Indian, there was a reserve and impenetrability about Thoreau which prevented him from ever becoming really confidential in print. If he had but unbended more frequently, and not sifted his thought so conscientiously before he gave us the benefit of it, he would certainly have appealed to our affections far more than he does.

One feels in comparing his writings with the accounts of him by friends how much that was interesting in the man remains unexpressed in terms of literature. Partly this is due, no doubt, to his being tormented with the idea of self-education that he had learnt from Emerson. In a philosopher and moralist self-education is all very well. But in a naturalist and in a writer with so much of the Vagabond about him as Thoreau this sensitiveness about self-culture, this anxiety to eliminate all the temperamental tares, is blameworthy.

The care he took to eliminate the lighter element in his work—the flash of wit, the jocose aside—a care which pursued him to the last, seems to show that he too often mistook gravity for seriousness. Like Dr. Watts' bee (which is not Maeterlinck's) he "improved the shining hour," instead of allowing the shining hour to carry with it its own improvement, none the less potent for being unformulated. But beside the Emersonian influence, there is the Puritan strain in Thoreau's nature, which must not be overlooked. No doubt it also is partly accountable for his literary silences and austere moods.

To revert to the Indians.

If Thoreau does not deal dramatically with his Indians, yet he had much that is interesting and suggestive to say about them. These are some passages from *A Week on the Concord*:—

> "We talk of civilizing the Indians, but that is not the name for his improvement. By the wary independence and aloofness of his dim forest-life he preserves his intercourse with his native gods, and is admitted from time to time to a rare and peculiar society with Nature. He has glances of starry recognition to which our salons are strangers. The steady illumination of his genius, dim only because distant, is like the faint but satisfying light of the stars compared with the dazzling but ineffectual and short-lived blaze of

candles. . . . We would not always be soothing and taming Nature, breaking the horse and the ox, but sometimes ride the horse wild and chase the buffalo. The Indian's intercourse with Nature is at least such as admits of the greatest independence of each. If he is somewhat of a stranger in her midst, the gardener is too much of a familiar. There is something vulgar and foul in the latter's closeness to his mistress, something noble and cleanly in the former's distance. In civilization, as in a southern latitude, man degenerates at length and yields to the incursion of more northern tribes.

'Some nations yet shut in
With hills of ice.'

"There are other savager and more primeval aspects of Nature than our poets have sung. It is only white man's poetry—Homer and Ossian even can never revive in London or Boston. And yet behold how these cities are refreshed by the mere tradition or the imperfectly transmitted fragrance and flavour of these wild fruits. If one could listen but for an instant to the chant of the Indian muse, we should understand why he will not exchange his savageness for civilization. Nations are not whimsical. Steel and blankets are strong temptations, but the Indian does well to continue Indian."

These are no empty generalizations, but the comments of a man who has observed closely and sympathetically. All of Thoreau's references to Indian life merit the closest attention. For, as I have said, they help to explain the man himself. He had a sufficient touch of wildness to be able to detach himself from the civilized man's point of view. Hence the life of the woods came so naturally to him. The luxuries, the excitements, that mean so much to some, Thoreau passed by indifferently. There is much talk to-day of "the simple life," and the phrase has become tainted with affectation. Often it means nothing more than a passing fad on the part of overfed society people who are anxious for a new sensation. A fad with a moral flavour about it will always commend itself to a certain section. Certainly it is quite innocuous, but, on the other hand, it is quite superficial. There is no real intention of living a simple life any more than there is any deep resolve on the part of the man who takes the Waters annually to abstain in the future from overeating. But with Thoreau the simple life was a vital reality. He was not devoid of American self-consciousness, and perhaps he pats himself on the back for his healthy tastes more often than we should like. But of his fundamental sincerity there can be no question.

He saw even more clearly than Emerson the futility and debilitating effect of extravagance and luxury—especially American luxury. And his whole life was an indignant protest.

Yet it is a mistake to think (as some do) that he favoured a kind of Rousseau-like "Return to Nature," without any regard to the conventions of civilization. "It is not," he states emphatically, "for a man to put himself in opposition to society, but to maintain himself in whatever attitude he finds himself through obedience to the laws of his own being, which will never be one of opposition to a just government. I left the woods for as good a reason as I went there. Perhaps it seemed to me that I had several more lives to live, and could not spare any more time for that one."

This is not the language of a crank, or the words of a man who, as Lowell unfairly said, seemed "to insist in public in going back to flint and steel when there is a match-box in his pocket."

Lowell's criticism of Thoreau, indeed, is quite wide of the mark. It assumes throughout that Thoreau aimed at "an entire independence of mankind," when Thoreau himself repeatedly says that he aimed at nothing of the sort. He made an experiment for the purpose of seeing what a simple, frugal, open-air life would do for him. The experiment being made, he returned quietly to the conditions of ordinary life. But he did not lack self-assurance, and his frank satisfaction with the results of his experiment was not altogether pleasing to those who had scant sympathy with his passion for the Earth.

To be quite fair to Lowell and other hostile critics one must admit that, genuine as Thoreau was, he had the habit common to all self-contained and self-opiniated men of talking at times as though his very idiosyncrasies were rules of conduct imperative upon others. His theory of life was sound enough, his demand for simple modes of living, for a closer communion with Nature, for a more sympathetic understanding of the "brute creation," were reasonable beyond question. But the Emersonian mannerism (which gives an appearance of dogmatism, when no dogmatism is intended) starts up from time to time and gives the reader the impression that the path to salvation traverses Walden, all other paths being negligible, and that you cannot attain perfection unless you keep a pet squirrel.

But if a sentence here and there has an annoying flavour of complacent dogmatism, and if the note of self-assertion grows too loud on occasion for our sensitive ears, [102] yet his life and writings considered as a whole do not assuredly favour verdicts so unfavourable as those of Lowell and Stevenson.

Swagger and exaggeration may be irritating, but after all the important thing is whether a man has anything to swagger about, whether the case which he exaggerates is at heart sane and just.

Every Vagabond swaggers because he is an egotist more or less, and relishes keenly the life he has mapped out for himself. But the swagger is of the harmless kind; it is not really offensive; it is a sort of childish exuberance that plays over the surface of his mind, without injuring it, the harmless vanity of one who having escaped from the schoolhouse of convention congratulates himself on his good luck.

Swagger of this order you will find in the writings even of that quiet, unassuming little man De Quincey. Hazlitt had no small measure of it, and certainly it meets us in the company of Borrow. It is very noticeable in Whitman—far more so than in Thoreau. Why then does this quality tend to exasperate more when we find it in *Walden*? Why has Thoreau's sincerity been impugned and Whitman escaped? Why are Thoreau's mannerisms greeted with angry frowns, and the mannerisms, say of Borrow, regarded with good-humoured intolerance? Chiefly, I think, because of Thoreau's desperate efforts to justify his healthy Vagabondage by Emersonian formulas.

I am not speaking of his sane and comprehensive philosophy of life. The Vagabond has his philosophy of life no less than the moralist, though as a rule he is content to let it lie implicit in his writings, and is not anxious to turn it into a gospel. But he did not always realize the difference between moral characteristics and temperamental peculiarities, and many of his admirers have done him ill service by trying to make of his very Vagabondage (admirable enough in its way) a rule of faith for all and sundry. Indeed, I think that much of the resentment expressed against Thoreau by level-headed critics is due to the unwise eulogy of friends.

Thoreau has become an object of worship to the crank, and in our annoyance with the crank—who is often a genuine reformer destitute of humour—we are apt to jumble up devotee and idol together. Idol-worship never does any good to the idol.

IV

As a thinker Thoreau is suggestive and stimulating, except when he tries to systematize. Naturally I think he had a discursive and inquisitive, rather than a profound and analytical mind. He was in sympathy with Eastern modes of regarding life; and the pantheistic tendency of his religious thought, especially his care and reverence for all forms of life, suggest the devout Buddhist. The varied references scattered throughout his writings to the Sacred Books of the East show how Orientalism affected him.

Herein we touch upon the most attractive side of the man; for it is this Orientalism, I think, in his nature that explains his regard for, and his sympathy with, the birds and animals.

The tenderness of the Buddhist towards the lower creation is not due to sentimentalism, nor is it necessarily a sign of sensitiveness of feeling. In his profoundly interesting study of the Burmese people Mr. Fielding Hall has summed up admirably the teaching of Buddha: "Be in love with all things, not only with your fellows, but with the whole world, with every creature that walks the earth, with the birds in the air, with the insects in the grass. All life is akin to man." The oneness of life is realized by the Eastern as it seldom is by the Western. The love that stirs in your heart kindled the flower into beauty, and broods in the great silent pools of the forest.

But Nature is not always kind. That he cannot help feeling. She inspires fear as well as love. She scatters peace and consolation, but can scatter also pain and death. All forms of life are more or less sacred. The creatures of the forest whose ferocity and cunning are manifest, may they not be inhabited by some human spirit that has misused his opportunities in life? Thus they have an affinity with us, and are signs of what we may become.

And if a measure of sacredness attaches to all life, however unfriendly and harmful it may seem, the gentler forms of life are especially to be objects of reverence and affection.

In one particular, however, Thoreau's attitude towards the earth and all that therein is differed from the Buddhist, inasmuch as the fear that enters into the Eastern's Earth-worship was entirely purged from his mind. Mr. Page has instituted a suggestive comparison between Thoreau and St. Francis d'Assisi. Certainly the rare magnetic attraction which Thoreau seemed to have exercised over his "brute friends" was quite as remarkable as the power attributed to St. Francis, and it is true to say that in both cases the sympathy for animals is constantly justified by a reference to a dim but real brotherhood. The brutes are "undeveloped men"; they await their transformation and stand on their defence; and it is very easy to see that inseparably bound up with this view there are certain elements of mysticism common to the early saint and the American "hut builder." [106]

And yet, perhaps, Mr. Page presses the analogy between the medieval saint and the American "poet-naturalist" too far. St. Francis had an ardent, passionate nature, and whether leading a life of dissipation or tending to the poor, there is about him a royal impulsiveness, a passionate abandonment, pointing to a temperament far removed from Thoreau's.

Prodigal in his charities, riotous in his very austerities, his tenderness towards the animals seems like the overflowing of a finely sensitive and artistic nature. With Thoreau one feels in the presence of a more tranquil, more self-contained spirit; his affection is the affection of a kindly scientist who is intensely interested in the ways and habits of birds, beasts, and fishes; one who does not give them the surplus of the love he bears towards his fellow-men so much as a care and love which he does not extend so freely towards his fellows. I do not mean that he was apathetic, especially when his fellow-creatures were in trouble; his eloquent defence of John Brown, his kindliness towards simple folk, are sufficient testimony on this score. But on the whole his interest in men and women was an abstract kind of interest; he showed none of the personal curiosity and eager inquisitiveness about them that he showed towards the denizens of the woods and streams. And if you are not heartily interested in your fellow-men you will not love them very deeply.

I am not sure that Hawthorne was so far out in his characterization "Donatello"—the creature half-animal, half-man, which he says was suggested by Thoreau. It does not pretend to realize all his characteristics, nor do justice to his fine qualities. None the less in its picture of a man with a flavour of the wild and untameable about him—whose uncivilized nature brings him into a close and vital intimacy with the animal world, we detect a real psychological affinity with Thoreau. May not Thoreau's energetic rebukes of the evils of civilization have received an added zest from his instinctive repugnance to many of the civilized amenities valued by the majority?

Many of Thoreau's admirers—including Mr. Page and Mr. Salt—defend him stoutly against the charge of unsociability, and they see in this feeling for the brute creation an illustration of his warm humanitarianism. "Thoreau loves the animals," says Mr. Page, "because they are manlike and seem to yearn toward human forms." It seems to me that Thoreau's affection was a much simpler affair than this. He was drawn towards them because *he* felt an affinity with them—an affinity more compelling in its attraction than the affinity of the average human person.

No doubt he felt, as Shelley did when he spoke of "birds and even insects" as his "kindred," that this affinity bespoke a wider brotherhood of feeling than men are usually ready to acknowledge. But this is not the same as loving animals *because* they are manlike. He loved them surely because they were *living* things, and he was drawn towards all living things, not because he detected any semblance to humankind in them. The difference between these two attitudes is not easy to define clearly; but it is a real, not a nominal difference.

It is argued, however, as another instance of Thoreau's undervalued sociability, that he was very fond of children. That he was fond of children may be admitted, and some of the pleasantest stories about him relate to his rambles with children. His huckleberry parties were justly famous, if report speaks true. "His resources for entertainment," says Mr. Moncure Conway, "were inexhaustible. He would tell stories of the Indians who once dwelt thereabouts till the children almost looked to see a red man skulking with his arrow and stone, and every plant or flower on the bank or in the water, and every fish, turtle, frog, lizard about was transformed by the wand of his knowledge from the low form into which the spell of our ignorance had reduced it into a mystic beauty."

Emerson and his children frequently accompanied him on these expeditions. "Whom shall we ask?" demanded Emerson's little daughter. "All children from six to sixty," replied her father.

> "Thoreau," writes Mr. Conway in his *Reminiscences*, "was the guide, for he knew the precise locality of every variety of berry."

> "Little Edward Emerson, on one occasion, carrying a basket of fine huckleberries, had a fall and spilt them all. Great was his distress, and offers of berries could not console him for the loss of those gathered by himself. But Thoreau came, put his arm round the troubled child, and explained to him that if the crop of huckleberries was to continue it was necessary that some should be scattered. Nature had provided that little boys and girls should now and then stumble and sow the berries. 'We shall,' he said, 'have a grand lot of bushes and berries on this spot, and we shall owe them to you.' Edward began to smile."

Thoreau evidently knew how to console a child, no less than how to make friends with a squirrel. But his fondness for children is no more an argument for his sociability, than his fondness for birds or squirrels. As a rule it will be found, I think, that a predilection for children is most marked in men generally reserved and inaccessible. Lewis Carroll, for instance, to take a famous recent example, was the reverse of a sociable man. Shy, reserved, even cold in ordinary converse, he would expand immediately when in the company of children. Certainly he understood them much better than he did their elders. Like Thoreau, moreover, Lewis Carroll was a lover of animals.

Social adaptability was not a characteristic of Thackeray, his moroseness and reserve frequently alienating people; yet no one was more devoted to children, or a more delightful friend to them.

So far from being an argument in favour of its possessor's sociability, it seems to be a tolerable argument against it. It is not hard to understand why. When analysed this fondness for children is much the same in quality as the fondness for animals. A man is drawn towards children because there is something fresh, unsophisticated, and elemental about them. It has no reference to their moral qualities, though the æsthetic element plays a share. Thoreau knew how to comfort little Edward Emerson just as he knew how to cheer the squirrel that sought a refuge in his waistcoat. This fondness, however, must not be confused with the paternal instinct. A man may desire to have children, realize that desire, interest himself in their welfare, and yet not be really fond of them. As children they may not attract him, but he regards them as possibilities for perpetuating the family and for enhancing its prestige.

A good deal of nonsense is talked about the purity and innocence of childhood. Children are consequently brought up in a morbidly sentimental atmosphere that makes of them too quickly little prigs or little hypocrites. I do not believe, however, that any man or woman who is genuinely fond of children is moved by this artificial point of view. The innocence and purity of children is a middle-class convention. None but the unreal sentimentalist really believes in it. What attracts us most in children is naturalness and simplicity. We note in them the frank predominance of the instinctive life, and they charm us in many ways just as young animals do.

Lewis Carroll's biographer speaks of "his intense admiration for the white innocence and uncontaminated spirituality of childhood."

If this be true then it shows that the Rev. C. L. Dodgson had a great deal to learn about children, who are, or should be, healthy little pagans. But though his liking for them may not have been free of the sentimental taint, there is abundant proof that other less debatable qualities in childhood appealed to him with much greater force.

"Uncontaminated spirituality," forsooth. I would as soon speak of the uncontaminated spirituality of a rabbit. I am sure rabbits are a good deal more lovable than some children.

Thoreau's love of children, then, seems to be only a fresh instance of his attraction towards simpler, more elemental forms of life. Men and women not ringed round by civilized conventions, children who have the freshness and wildness of the woods about them; such were the human beings that interested him.

Such an attitude has its advantages as well as its limitations. It calls neither for the censorious blame visited upon Thoreau by some of the critics nor the indiscriminate eulogy bestowed on him by others.

The Vagabond who withdraws himself to any extent from the life of his day, who declines to conform to many of its arbitrary conventions, escapes much of the fret and tear, the heart-aching and the disillusionment that others share in. He retains a freshness, a simplicity, a joyfulness, not vouchsafed to those who stay at home and never wander beyond the prescribed limits. He exhibits an individuality which is more genuinely the legitimate expression of his temperament. It is not warped, crossed, suppressed, as many are.

And this is why the literary Vagabond is such excellent company, having wandered from the beaten track he has much to tell others of us who have stayed at home. There is a wild luxuriance about his character that is interesting and fascinating—if you are not thrown for too long in his company. The riotous growth of eccentricities and idiosyncrasies are picturesque enough, though you must expect to find thorns and briars.

On the other hand, we must beware of sentimentalizing the Vagabond, and to present him as an ideal figure—as some enthusiasts have done—seems to me a mistake. As a wholesome bitter corrective to the monotonous sweet of civilization he is admirable enough. Of his tonic influence in literature there can be no question. But it is well for the Vagabond to be in the minority. Perhaps these considerations should come at the close of the series of Vagabond studies, but they arise naturally when considering Thoreau—for Thoreau is one of the few Vagabonds whom his admirers have tried to canonize. Not content with the striking qualities which the Vagabond naturally exhibits, some of his admirers cannot rest without dragging in other qualities to which he has no claim. Why try to prove that Thoreau was really a most sociable character, that Whitman was the profoundest philosopher of his day, that Jefferies was—deep down—a conventionally religious man? Why, oh why, may we not leave them in their pleasant wildness without trying to make out that they were the best company in the world for five-o'clock teas and chapel meetings?

For—and it is well to admit it frankly—the Vagabond loses as well as gains by his deliberate withdrawal from the world. No man can live to himself without some injury to his character. The very cares and worries, the checks and clashings, consequent on meeting other individualities tend to keep down the egotistic elements in a man's nature. The necessary give and take, the sacrifice of self-interests, the little abnegations, the moral adjustment following the appreciation of other points of view; all these things are good for men and women. Yes, and it is good even to mix with very conventional people—I do not say live with them—however distasteful it may be, for the excessive caution, the prudential, opportunistic qualities they exhibit, serve a useful purpose in the scheme of things. The ideal thing, no doubt, is to mix with as many types, as many varieties of the human species, as possible. Browning owes his great power as a poet to his tireless interest in all sorts and conditions of men and women.

It is idle to pretend then that Thoreau lost nothing by his experiments, and by the life he fashioned for himself. Nature gives us plenty of choice; we are invited to help ourselves, but everything must be paid for. There are drawbacks as well as compensations; and the most a man can do is to strike a balance.

And in Thoreau's case the balance was a generous one.

Better than his moralizing, better than his varied culture, was his intimacy with Nature. Moralists are plentiful, scholars abound, but men in close, vital sympathy with the Earth, a sympathy that comprehends because it loves, and loves because it comprehends, are rare. Let us make the most of them.

In one of his most striking Nature poems Mr. George Meredith exclaims:—

> "Enter these enchanted woods,
>   You who dare.
> Nothing harms beneath the leaves
> More than waves a swimmer cleaves.
> Toss your heart up with the lark,
> Foot at peace with mouse and worm,
>   Fair you fare,
> Only at a dread of dark
> Quaver, and they quit their form:
> Thousand eyeballs under hoods
>   Have you by the hair.
> Enter these enchanted woods,
>   You who dare."

So to understand Nature you must trust her, otherwise she will remain at heart fearsome and cryptic.

> "You must love the light so well
> That no darkness will seem fell;
> Love it so you could accost
> Fellowly a livid ghost."

Mr. Meredith requires us to approach Nature with an unswerving faith in her goodness.

No easy thing assuredly; and to some minds this attitude will express a facile optimism. Approve it or reject it, however, as we may, 'tis a philosophy that can claim many and diverse adherents, for it is no dusty formula of academic thought, but a message of the sunshine and the winds. Talk of suffering and death to the Vagabond, and he will reply as did Petulengro, "Life is sweet, brother." Not that he ignores other matters, but it is sufficient for him that "life is sweet." And after all he speaks as to what he has known.

V
ROBERT LOUIS STEVENSON

"Choice word and measured phrase above the reach
Of ordinary man."

WORDSWORTH (*Revolution and Independence*).

"Variety's the very spice of life
That gives it all its flavour."

COWPER.

... "In his face,
There shines a brilliant and romantic grace,
A spirit intense and rare, with trace on trace
Of passion and impudence and energy.
Valiant in velvet, light in ragged luck,
Most vain, most generous, sternly critical,
Buffoon and poet, lover and sensualist:
A deal of Ariel, just a streak of Puck,
Much Antony, of Hamlet most of all,
And something of the Shorter Catechist.

W. E. HENLEY.

I

Romance! At times it passes athwart our vision, yet no sooner seen than gone; at times it sounds in our ears, only to tremble into silence ere we realize it; at times it touches our lips, and is felt in the blood, but our outstretched arms gather naught but the vacant air. The scent of a flower, the splendour of a sunrise, the glimmer of a star, and it wakens into being. Sometimes when standing in familiar places, speaking on matters of every day, suddenly, unexpectedly, it manifests its presence. A turn of the head, a look in the eye, an inflection of the voice, and this strange, indefinable thing stirs within us. Or, it may be, we are alone, traversing some dusty highway of thought, when in a flash some long-forgotten memory starts at our very feet, and we realize that Romance is alive.

I would fain deem Romance a twin—a brother and sister. The one fair and radiant with the sunlight, strong and clean-fibred, warm of blood and joyous of spirit; a creature of laughter and delight. I would fancy him regarding the world with clear, shining eyes, faintly parted lips, a buoyant expectancy in every line of his tense figure. Ready for anything and everything; the world opening up before him like a white, alluring road; tasting curiously every adventure, as a man plucks fruit by the wayside, knowing no horizon to his outlook, no end to his journey, no limit to his enterprise.

As such I see one of the twins. And the other? Dark and wonderful; the fragrance of poesy about her hair, the magic of mystery in her unfathomable eyes. Sweet is her voice and her countenance is comely. A creature of moonlight and starshine. She follows in the wake of her brother; but his ways are not her ways. Away, out of sound of his mellow laughter, she is the spirit that haunts lonely places. There is no price by which you may win her, no entreaty to which she will respond. Compel her you cannot, woo her you may not. Yet, uninvited, unbidden, she will steal into the garret, gaunt in its lonesome ugliness, and bend over the wasted form of some poor literary hack, until his dreams reflect the beauty of her presence.

And yet, when one's fancy has run riot in order to recall Romance, how much

remains that cannot be put into words. One thing, however, is certain. Romance must be large and generous enough to comprehend the full-blooded geniality of a Scott, the impalpable mystery of a Coleridge or Shelley, to extend a hand to the sun-tanned William Morris, and the lover of twilight, Nathaniel Hawthorne.

Borrow was a Romantic, so is Stevenson. Scott was a Romantic, likewise Edgar Allan Poe. If Romance be not a twin, then it must change its form and visage wondrously to appeal to temperaments so divergent. But if Romance be a twin (the conceit will serve our purpose) then one may realize how Scott and Borrow followed in the brother's wake; Stevenson and Poe being drawn rather towards the sister.

In the case of Stevenson it may seem strange that one who wrote stirring adventures, who delighted boys of all ages with *Treasure Island* and *Black Arrow* (oh, excellent John Silver!), and followed in the steps of Sir Walter in *The Master of Ballantrae* and *Catriona*, should not be associated with the adventurous brother. But Scott and Stevenson have really nothing in common, beyond a love for the picturesque—and there is nothing distinctive in that. It is an essential qualification in the equipment of every Romantic. Adventures, as such, did not appeal to Stevenson, I think; it was the spice of mystery in them that attracted him. Watch him and you will find he is not content until he has thrown clouds of phantasy over his pictures. His longer stories have no unity—they are disconnected episodes strung lightly together, and this is why his short stories impress us far more with their power and brilliance.

Markheim and *Jekyll and Hyde* do not oppress the imagination in the same way as do Poe's tales of horror; but they show the same passion for the dark corners of life, the same fondness for the gargoyles of Art. This is Romance on its mystic side.

Throughout his writings—I say nothing of his letters, which stand in a different category—one can hear

> "The horns of Elfland faintly blowing."

Sometimes the veil of phantasy is shaken by a peal of impish laughter, as if he would say, "Lord, what fools these mortals be!" but the attitude that persists—breaks there must be, and gusty moods, or it would not be Stevenson—is the attitude of the Romantic who loves rather the night side of things.

II

Much has been written about the eternal boy in Stevenson. I confess that this does not strike me as a particularly happy criticism. In a superficial sort of way it is, of course, obvious enough; he was fond of "make-believe"; took a boyish delight in practical joking; was ever ready for an adventure. But so complex and diverse his temperament that it is dangerous to seize on one aspect and say, "There is the real Stevenson." Ariel, Hamlet, and the Shorter Catechist cross and recross his pages as we read them. Probably each reader of Stevenson retains most clearly one special phase. It is the Ariel in Stevenson that outlasts for me the other moods. If any one phase can be said to strike the keynote of his temperament, it is the whimsical, freakish, but kindly Ariel—an Ariel bound in service to the Prospero of fiction—never quite happy, longing for his freedom, yet knowing that he must for a while serve his master. One can well understand why John Addington Symonds dubbed Stevenson "sprite." This elfish dement in Stevenson is most apparent in his letters and stories.

The figures in his stories are less flesh-and-blood persons than the shapes—some gracious, some terrifying—that the Ariel world invoke. It is not that Stevenson had no grip on reality; his grip-hold on life was very firm and real. Beneath the light badinage, the airy, graceful wit that plays over his correspondence, there is a steel-like tenacity. But in his stories he leaves the solid earth for a phantastic world of his own. He does so deliberately: he turns his back on reality, has dealings with phantom passions. His historical romances are like ghostly editions of Scott. There is light, but little heat in his fictions. They charm our fancy, but do not seize upon our imagination. Stevenson's novels remind one of an old *Punch* joke about the man who chose a wife to match his furniture. Stevenson chooses his personages to match his furniture—his cunningly-woven tapestries of style; and the result is that we are too conscious of the tapestry on the wall, too little conscious of the people who move about the rooms. If only Stevenson had suited his style to his matter, as he does in his letters, which are written in fine Vagabond spirit—his romances would have seemed less artificial. I say *seemed*, for it was the stylist that stood in the way of the story-teller. Stevenson's sense of character was keen enough, particularly in his ripe, old "disreputables." But much of his remarkable psychology was lost, it seems to me, by the lack of dramatic presentment.

Borrow's characters do not speak Borrow so emphatically as do Stevenson's characters speak Stevenson. And with Stevenson it matters more. Borrow's picturesque, vivid, but loose, loquacious style, fits his subject-matter on the whole very well. But Stevenson's delicate, nervous, mannerized style suits but ill some of the scenes he is describing. If it suits, it suits by a happy accident, as in the delightful sentimentality, *Providence and the Guitar*.

To appraise Stevenson's merits as a Romantic one has to read him after reading Scott, Dumas, Victor Hugo; or, better still, to peruse these giants after dallying with Ariel.

We realize then what it is that we had vaguely missed in Stevenson—the human touch. These men believe in the figments of their imagination, and make us believe in them.

Stevenson is obviously sceptical as to their reality; we can almost see a furtive smile upon his lip as he writes. But there is nothing unreal about the man, whatever we feel of the Artist.

In his critical comments on men and matters, especially when Hamlet and the Shorter Catechist come into view, we shall find a vigorous sanity, a shrewd yet genial outlook, that seems to say there is no make-believe *here*;

here I am not merely amusing myself; here, honestly and heartily admitted, you may find the things that life has taught me.

III

Stevenson had many sides, but there were two especially that reappear again and again, and were the controlling forces in his nature. One was the Romantic element, the other the Artistic. It may be thought that these twain have much in common; but it is not so. In poetry the first gives us a Blake, a Shelley; the second a Keats, a Tennyson. Variety, fresh points of view, these are the breath of life to the Romantic. But for the Artist there is one constant, unchanging ideal. The Romantic ventures out of sheer love of the venture, the other out of sheer love for some definite end in view. It is not usual to find them coexisting as they did in Stevenson, and their dual existence gives an added piquancy and interest to his work. It is the Vagabond Romantic in him that leads him into so many byways and secret places, that sends him airily dancing over the wide fields of literature; ever on the move, making no tabernacle for himself in any one grove. And it is the Artist who gives that delicacy of finish, that exquisite nicety of touch, to the veriest trifle that he essays. The matter may be beggarly, the manner is princely.

Mark the high ideal he sets before him: "The Artist works entirely upon honour. The Public knows little or nothing of those merits in its quest of which you are condemned to spend the bulk of your endeavours. Merits of design, the merit of first-hand energy, the merit of a certain cheap accomplishment, which a man of the artistic temper easily acquires; these they can recognize, and these they value. But to those more exquisite refinements of proficiency and finish, which the Artist so ardently desires and so keenly feels, for which (in the vigorous words of Balzac) he must toil 'like a miner buried in a landslip,' for which day after day he recasts and revises and rejects, the gross mass of the Public must be ever blind. To those lost pains, suppose you attain the highest point of merit, posterity may possibly do justice; suppose, as is so probable, that you fail by even a hair's breadth of the highest, rest certain they shall never be observed. Under the shadow of this cold thought alone in his studio the Artist must preserve from day to day his constancy to the ideal." [124a]

An exacting ideal, but one to which Stevenson was as faithful as a Calvinist to his theology. The question arises, however; is the fastidiousness, the patient care of the Artist, consistent with Vagabondage? Should one not say the greater the stylist, the lesser the Vagabond?

This may be admitted. And thus it is that in the letters alone do we find the Vagabond temperament of Stevenson fully asserting itself. Elsewhere 'tis held in check. As Mr. Sidney Colvin justly says: [124b] "In his letters—

excepting a few written in youth, and having more or less the character of exercises, and a few in after years which were intended for the public eye—Stevenson, the deliberate artist is scarcely forthcoming at all. He does not care a fig for order, or logical sequence, or congruity, or for striking a key of expression and keeping it, but becomes simply the most spontaneous and unstudied of human beings. He will write with the most distinguished eloquence on one day, with simple good sense and good feeling on a second, with flat triviality on another, and with the most slashing, often ultra-colloquial vehemency on a fourth, or will vary through all these moods, and more, in one and the same letter."

Fresh and spontaneous his letters invariably appear; with a touch of the invalid's nervous haste, but never lacking in courage, and with nothing of the querulousness which we connect with chronic ill-health. Weak and ailing, shadowed by death for many years before the end, Stevenson showed a fine fortitude, which will remain in the memory of his friends as his most admirable character. With the consistency of Mark Tapley (and with less talk about it) he determined to be jolly in all possible circumstances. Right to the end his wonderful spirits, his courageous gaiety attended him; the frail body grew frailer, but the buoyant intellect never failed him, or if it did so the failure was momentary, and in a moment he was recovered.

No little of his popularity is due to the desperate valour with which he contested the ground with death, inch by inch, and died, as Buckle and John Richard Green had done, in the midst of the work that he would not quit. Romance was by him to the last, gladdening his tired body with her presence; and if towards the end weariness and heart-sickness seized him for a spell, yet the mind soon resumed its mastery over weakness. In a prayer which he had written shortly before his death he had petitioned: "Give us to awake with smiles, give us to labour smiling; as the sun lightens the world, so let our lovingkindness make bright this house of our habitation." Assuredly in his case this characteristic petition had been realized; the prevalent sunniness of his disposition attended him to the last.

IV

Of all our writers there has been none to whom the epithet "charming" has been more frequently applied. Of late the epithet has become a kind of adjectival maid-of-all-work, and has done service where a less emphatic term would have done far better. But in Stevenson's case the epithet is fully justified. Of all the literary Vagabonds he is the most captivating. Not the most interesting; the most arresting, one may admit. There is greater power in Hazlitt; De Quincey is more unique; the "prophetic scream" of Whitman is more penetrating. But not one of them was endowed with such wayward graces of disposition as Stevenson. Whatever you read of his you think invariably of the man. Indeed the personal note in his work is frequently the most interesting thing about it. I mean that what attracts and holds us is often not any originality, any profundity, nothing specially inherent in the matter of his speech, but a bewitchingly delightful manner.

Examine his attractive essays, *Virginibus Puerisque* and *Familiar Studies of Men and Books*, and this quality will manifest itself. There is no pleasanter essay than the one on "Walking Tours"; it dresses up wholesome truths with so pleasant and picturesque a wit; it is so whimsical, yet withal so finely suggestive, that the reader who cannot yield to its fascination should consult a mental specialist.

For instance:—

> "It must not be imagined that a walking tour, as some would have us fancy, is merely a better or worse way of seeing the country. There are many ways of seeing landscape quite as good; and none more vivid, in spite of canting dilettantes, than from a railway train. But landscape on a walking tour is quite accessory. He who is indeed of the brotherhood does not voyage in quest of the picturesque, but of certain jolly humours—of the hope and spirit with which the march begins at morning, and the peace and spiritual repletion of the evening's rest. He cannot tell whether he puts his knapsack on or takes it off with more delight. The excitement of the departure puts him in key for that of the arrival. Whatever he does will be further rewarded in the sequel; and so pleasure leads on to pleasure in an endless chain."

An admirable opening, full of the right relish. And the wit and relish are maintained down to the last sentence. But it cannot fail to awaken memories of the great departed in the reader of books. "Now to be properly enjoyed," counsels Stevenson, "a walking tour should be gone upon alone. . . . a walking tour should be gone upon alone because freedom is of the essence," and so on in the same vein for twenty or thirty lines. One immediately recalls Hazlitt—"On Going a Journey": "One of the pleasantest things is going on a journey; but I like to go by myself. . . . The soul of a journey is liberty, perfect liberty, to think, feel, do just as one pleases."

A suspicion seizes the mind of the reader, and he will smile darkly to himself. But Stevenson is quite ready for him. "A strong flavour of Hazlitt, you think?" he seems to say, then with the frank ingenuousness of one who has confessed to "playing the sedulous ape," he throws in a quotation from this very essay of Hazlitt's and later on gives us more Hazlitt. It is impossible to resent it; it is so openly done, there is such a charming effrontery about the whole thing. And yet, though much that he says is obviously inspired by Hazlitt, he will impart that flavour of his own less mordant personality to the discourse.

If you turn to another, the "Truth of Intercourse," it is hard to feel that it would have thrived had not Elia given up his "Popular Fallacies." There is an unmistakable echo in the opening paragraph: "Among sayings that have a currency, in spite of being wholly false upon the face of them, for the sake of a half-truth upon another subject which is accidentally combined with the error, one of the grossest and broadest conveys the monstrous proposition that it is easy to tell the truth and hard to tell a lie. I wish heartily it were!" Similarly in other essays the influence of Montaigne is strongly felt; and although Stevenson never fails to impart the flavour of his own individuality to his discourses—for he is certainly no mere copyist—one realizes the unwisdom of those enthusiastic admirers who have bracketed him with Lamb, Montaigne, and Hazlitt. These were men of the primary order; whereas Stevenson with all his grace and charm is assuredly of the secondary order. And no admiration for his attractive personality and captivating utterances should blind us to this fact.

As a critic of books his originality is perhaps more pronounced, but wise and large though many of his utterances are, here again it is the pleasant wayward Vagabond spirit that gives salt and flavour to them. There are many critics less brilliant, less attractive in their speech, in whose judgment I should place greater reliance. Sometimes, as in the essay on "Victor Hugo's Romances," his own temperament stands in the way; at other times, as in his "Thoreau" article, there is a vein of wilful capriciousness, even of impish malice, that distorts his judgment. Neither essays can be passed over; in each there is power and shrewd flashes of discernment, and both are extremely interesting. One cannot say they are satisfying. Stevenson does scant justice to the extraordinary passion, the Titanic strength, of Hugo; and in the case of Thoreau he dwells too harshly upon the less gracious aspects of the "poet-naturalist."

It is only fair to say, however, that in the case of Thoreau he made generous amends in the preface to the Collected Essays. Both the reconsidered verdict and the original essay are highly characteristic of the man. Other men have said equally harsh things of Thoreau. Stevenson alone had the fairness, the frank, childlike spirit to go back upon himself. These are the things that endear us to Stevenson, and make it impossible to be angry with any of his paradoxes and extravagant capers. Who but Stevenson would have written thus: "The most temperate of living critics once marked a passage of my own with a cross and the words, 'This seems nonsense.' It not only seemed, it was so. It was a private bravado of my own which I had so often repeated to keep up my spirits that I had grown at last wholly to believe it, and had ended by setting it down as a contribution to the theory of life."

Touched by this confidence, one reads Stevenson—especially the letters—with a more discerning eye, a more compassionate understanding; and if at times one feels the presence of the Ariel too strong, and longs for a more human, less elfin personality, then the thought that we are dealing with deliberate "bravado" may well check our impatience.

Men who suffer much are wont to keep up a brave front by an appearance of indifference.

V

To turn now to another side of Stevenson—Stevenson the Artist, the artificer of phrases, the limner of pictures. His power here is shown in a threefold manner—in deft and happy phrasing, in skilful characterization, in delicately suggestive scenic descriptions.

This, for instance, as an instance of the first:—

> "The victim begins to shrink spiritually; he develops a fancy for parlours with a regulated atmosphere, and takes his morality on the principle of tin shoes and tepid milk. The care of one important body or soul becomes so engrossing that all the noises of the outer world begin to come thin and faint into the parlour with the regulated temperature; and the tin shoes go equally forward over blood and ruin" (*New Arabian Nights*).

Or this:—

> "Whitman, like a large, shaggy dog, just unchained, scouring the beaches of the world, and baying at the moon" (*Men and Books*).

Or this:—

> "To have a catchword in your mouth is not the same thing as to hold an opinion; still less is it the same thing as to have made one for yourself. There are too many of these catchwords in the world for people to rap out upon you like an oath by way of an argument. They have a currency as intellectual counters, and many respectable persons pay their way with nothing else" (*Virginibus Puerisque*).

In his characterization he is at his best—like Scott and Borrow—when dealing with the picaresque elements in life. His rogues are depicted with infinite gusto and admirable art, and although even they, in common with most of his characters, lack occasionally in substance and objective reality, yet when he has to illustrate a characteristic he will do so with a sure touch.

Take, for instance, this sketch of Herrick in *The Ebb Tide*—the weak, irresolute rascal, with just force enough to hate himself. He essays to end his ignominious career in the swift waters:—

> ... "Let him lie down with all races and generations of men in the house of sleep. It was easy to say, easy to do. To stop swimming; there was no mystery in that, if he could do it. Could he?
>
> "And he could not. He knew it instantly. He was instantly aware of an opposition in his members, unanimous and invincible, clinging to life with a single and fixed resolve, finger by finger, sinew by sinew; something that was at once he and not he—at once within and without him; the shutting of some miniature valve within the brain, which a single manly thought would suffice to open—and the grasp of an external fate ineluctable to gravity. To any man there may come at times a consciousness that there blows, through all the articulations of his body, the wind of a spirit not wholly his; that his mind rebels; that another girds him, and carries him whither he would not. It came even to Herrick with the authority of a revelation—there was no escape possible. The open door was closed in his recreant face. He must go back into the world and amongst men without illusion. He must stagger on to the end with the pack of his responsibility and disgrace, until a cold, a blow—a merciful chance blow—or the more merciful hangman should dismiss him from his infamy.
>
> "There were men who could commit suicide; there were men who could not; and he was one who could not. His smile was tragic. He could have spat upon himself."

Profoundly dissimilar in many ways, one psychological link binds together Dickens, Browning, and Stevenson—a love of the grotesque, a passion for the queer, phantastic sides of life. Each of them relished the tang of roughness, and in Browning's case the relish imparts itself to his style. Not so with Stevenson. He will delve with the others for curious treasure; but not until it is fairly wrought and beaten into a thing of finished beauty will he allow you to get a glimpse of it.

This is different from Browning, who will fling his treasures at you with all the mud upon them. But I am not sure that Stevenson's is always the better way. He may save you soiling your fingers; but the real attractiveness of certain things is inseparable from their uncouthness, their downright ugliness. Sometimes you feel that a plainer setting would have shown off the jewel to better advantage. Otherwise one has nothing but welcome for such memorable figures as John Silver, the Admiral in *The Story of a Lie*, Master Francis Villon, and a goodly company beside.

It is impossible even in such a cursory estimate of Stevenson as this to pass over his vignettes of Nature. And it is the more necessary to emphasize these, inasmuch as the Vagabond's passion for the Earth is clearly discernible in these pictures. They are no Nature sketches as imagined by a mere "ink-bottle feller"—to use a phrase of one of Mr. Hardy's rustics. One of Stevenson's happiest recollections was an "open air" experience when he slept on the earth. He loved the largeness of the open air, and his intense joy in natural sights and sounds bespeaks the man of fine, even hectic sensibility, whose nerves quiver for the benison of the winds and sunshine.

Ever since the days of Mrs. Radcliffe, who used the stormier aspects of Nature with such effect in her stories, down to Mr. Thomas Hardy, whose massive scenic effects are so remarkable, Nature has been regarded as a kind of "stage property" by the novelist.

To the great writers the Song of the Earth has proved an inspiration only second to the "Song of Songs," and the lesser writer has imitated as best he could so effective a decoration. But there is no mistaking the genuine lover of the Earth. He does not—as Oscar Wilde wittily said of a certain popular novelist—"frighten the evening sky into violent chromo-lithographic effects"; he paints the sunrises and sunsets with a loving fidelity which there is no mistaking. Nor are all the times and seasons of equal interest in his eyes. If we look back at the masters of fiction (ay, and mistresses too) in the past age, we shall note how each one has his favourite aspect, how each responds more readily to one special mood of the ancient Earth.

Mention has been made of Mrs. Radcliffe. Extravagant and absurd as her stories are in many ways, she was a genuine lover of Nature, especially of its grand and sublime aspects. Her influence may be traced in Scott, still more in Byron. The mystic side of Nature finds its lovers chiefly in the poets, in Coleridge and in Shelley. But at a later date Nathaniel Hawthorne found in the mysticism of the Earth his finest inspiration; while throughout the novels of Charlotte and Emily Brontë wail the bleak winds of the North, and the grey storm-clouds are always hurrying past. Even in Dickens there is more snow than sunshine, and we hear more of "the winds that would be howling at all hours" than of the brooding peace and quiet of summer days. Charles Kingsley is less partial towards the seasons, and cares less about the mysticism than the physical influences of Nature.

In our own day Mr. George Meredith has reminded us of the big geniality of the Earth; and the close relationship of the Earth and her moods with those who live nearest to her has found a faithful observer in Mr. Hardy.

Stevenson differs from Meredith and Hardy in this. He looks at her primarily with the eye of the artist. They look at her primarily with the eye of the scientific philosopher.

Here is a twilight effect from *The Return of the Native*:—

> "The sombre stretch of rounds and hollows seemed to rise and meet the evening gloom in pure sympathy, the heath exhaling darkness as rapidly as the heavens precipitated it. . . . The place became full of a watchful intentness now; for when other things sank brooding to sleep, the heath appeared slowly to awake and listen. Every night its Titanic form seemed to await something; but it had waited thus unmoved during so many centuries, through the crises of so many things, that it could only be imagined to await one last crisis—the final overthrow. . . . Twilight combined with the scenery of Egdon Heath to evolve a thing majestic without severity, impressive without showiness, emphatic in its admonitions, grand in its simplicity."

Contrast with this a twilight piece from Stevenson:—

> "The sky itself was of a ruddy, powerful, nameless changing colour, dark and glossy like a serpent's back. The stars by innumerable millions stuck boldly forth like lamps. The milky way was bright, like a moonlit cloud; half heaven seemed milky way. The greater luminaries shone each more clearly than a winter's moon. Their light was dyed in every sort of colour—red, like fire; blue, like steel; green, like the tracks of sunset; and so sharply did each stand forth in its own lustre that there was no appearance of that flat, star-spangled arch we know so well in pictures, but all the hollow of heaven was one chaos of contesting luminaries—a hurly-burly of stars. Against this the hill and rugged tree-tops stood out redly dark."

Each passage has a fresh beauty that removes it from the perfunctory tributes of the ordinary writer. But the difference between the Artist and the Philosopher is obvious. Not that Mr. Hardy has no claims as an artist. Different as their styles are, and although Stevenson has a more fastidious taste for words, the large, deliberate, massive art of Hardy is equally effective in its fashion. That, however, by the way. The point is that Mr.

Hardy never rests *as* an artist—he is quite as concerned with the philosophic as with the pictorial aspects of the scene. Stevenson rejoices as a Romantic; admires like an Artist.

VI

But if Stevenson does not care to philosophize over Nature—herein parting company with Thoreau as well as Hardy—he can moralize on occasion, and with infinite relish too.

"Something of the Shorter Catechist," as his friend Henley so acutely said. There is the Moralist in his essays, in some of the short stories—*Jekyll and Hyde* is a morality in disguise, and unblushingly so is *A Christmas Sermon*.

Some of his admirers have deplored this tendency in Stevenson; have shaken their heads gloomily over his Scottish ancestry, and spoken as apologetically about the moralizing as if it had been kleptomania.

Well, there it is as glaring and apparent as Borrow's big green gamp or De Quincey's insularity. "What business has a Vagabond to moralize?" asks the reader. Yet there is a touch of the Moralist in every Vagabond (especially the English-speaking Vagabond), and its presence in Stevenson gives an additional piquancy to his work. The *Lay Morals* and the *Christmas Sermon* may not exhilarate some readers greatly, but there is a fresher note, a larger utterance in the *Fables*. And even if you do not care for Stevenson's "Hamlet" and "Shorter Catechist" moods, is it wise, even from the artistic point of view, to wish away that side of his temperament? Was it the absence of the "Shorter Catechist" in Edgar Allan Poe that sent him drifting impotently across the world, brilliant, unstable, aspiring, grovelling; a man of many fine qualities and extraordinary intensity of imagination, but tragically weak where he ought to have been strong? And was it the "Shorter Catechist" in Stevenson that gave him that grip-hold of life's possibilities, imbued him with his unfailing courage, and gave him as Artist a strenuous devotion to an ideal that accompanied him to the end? Or was it so lamentable a defect as certain critics allege? I wonder.

VI
RICHARD JEFFERIES

"Noises of river and of grove
And moving things in field and stall
And night birds' whistle shall be all
Of the world's speech that we shall hear."

WILLIAM MORRIS.

"The poetry of earth is never dead."

KEATS.

I

The longing of a full, sensuous nature for fairer dreams of beauty than come within its ken; the delight of a passionate soul in the riotous wealth of the Earth, the luxuriant prodigality of the Earth; the hysterical joy of the invalid in the splendid sanity of the sunlight—these are the sentiments that well up from the writings of Richard Jefferies.

By comparison with him, Thoreau's Earth-worship seems quite a stolid affair, and even Borrow's frank enjoyment of the open air has a strangely apathetic touch about it.

No doubt he felt more keenly than did the Hermit of Walden, or the Norfolk giant, but it was not so much passionate intensity as nervous susceptibility. He had the sensitive quivering nerves of the neurotic which respond to the slightest stimulus. Of all the "Children of the Open Air" Jefferies was the most sensitive; but for all that I would not say that he felt more deeply than Thoreau, Borrow, or Stevenson.

Some people are especially susceptible by constitution to pain or pleasure, but it would be rash to assume hastily that on this account they have more deeply emotional natures. That they express their feelings more readily is no guarantee that they feel more deeply.

In other words, there is a difference between susceptibility and passion.

Whether a man has passion—be it of love or hate—can be judged only by his general attitude towards his fellow-beings, and by the stability of the emotion.

Now Jefferies certainly had keener sympathies with humankind than Thoreau, and these sympathies intensified as the years rolled by. Few men have espoused more warmly the cause of the agricultural labourer. Perhaps Hodge has never experienced a kinder advocate than Jefferies. To accuse him of superficiality of emotion would be unfair; for he was a man with much natural tenderness in his disposition.

All that I wish to protest against is the assumption made by some that because he has written so feelingly about Hodge, because he has shown so quick a response to the beauties of the natural world, he was therefore gifted with a deep nature, as has been claimed for him by some of his admirers.

One of the characteristics that differentiates the Vagabond writer from his fellows is, I think, a lack of passion—always excepting a passion for the earth, a quality lacking human significance. In their human sympathies they vary: but in no case, not even with Whitman, as I hope to show in my next paper, is there a *passion* for humankind. There may be curiosity about certain types, as with Borrow and Stevenson; a delight in simple natures, as with Thoreau; a broad, genial comradeship with all and sundry, as in the case of Whitman; but never do you find depth, intensity.

Jefferies then presents to my mind all the characteristics of the Vagabond, his many graces and charms, his notable deficiencies, especially the absence of emotional stability. This trait is, of course, more pronounced in some Vagabonds than in others; but it belongs to his inmost being. Eager, curious, adventurous; tasting this experience and that; his emotions share with his intellect in a chronic restless transition. More easily felt than defined is the lack of permanence in his nature; his emotions flame fitfully and in gusts, rather than with steady persistence. Finally, despite the tenderness and kindliness he can show, the egotistic elements absorb too much of his nature. A great egotist can never be a great lover.

This may seem a singularly ungracious prelude to a consideration of Richard Jefferies; but whatever it may seem it is quite consistent with a hearty admiration for his genius, and a warm appreciation of the man. Passion he had of a kind, but it was the rapt, self-centred passion of the mystic.

He interests us both as an artist and as a thinker. It will be useful, therefore, to keep these points of view as separate as possible in studying his writings.

II

Looking at him first of all as an artist, the most obvious thing that strikes a reader is his power to convey sensuous impressions. He loved the Earth, not as some have done with the eye or ear only, but with every nerve of his body. His scenic pictures are more glowing, more ardent than those of Thoreau. There was more of the poet, less of the naturalist in Jefferies. Perhaps it would have been juster to call Thoreau a poetic naturalist, and reserved the term poet-naturalist for Jefferies. Be that as it may, no one can read Jefferies—especially such books as *Wild Life in a*

Southern County, or *The Life of the Fields*, without realizing the keen sensibility of the man to the sensuous impressions of Nature.

Again and again in reading Jefferies one is reminded of the poet Keats. There is the same physical frailty of constitution and the same rare susceptibility to every manifestation of beauty. There is, moreover, the same intellectual devotion to beauty which made Keats declare Truth and Beauty to be one. And the likeness goes further still.

The reader who troubles to compare the sensuous imagery of the three great Nature poets—Wordsworth, Shelley, and Keats, will realize an individual difference in apprehending the beauties of the natural world. Wordsworth worships with his ear, Shelley with his eye, Keats with his sense of touch. Sound, colour, feeling—these things inform the poetry of these great poets, and give them their special individual charm.

Now, in Jefferies it is not so much the colour of life, or the sweet harmonies of the Earth, that he celebrates, though of course these things find a place in his prose songs. It is the "glory of the sum of things" that diffuses itself and is felt by every nerve in his body.

Take, for instance, the opening to *Wild Life in a Southern County*:—

> "The inner slope of the green fosse is inclined at an angle pleasant to recline on, with the head just below the edge, in the summer sunshine. A faint sound as of a sea heard in a dream—a sibilant "sish-sish"—passes along outside, dying away and coming again as a fresh wave of the wind rushes through the bennets and the dry grass. There is the happy hum of bees—who love the hills—as they speed by laden with their golden harvest, a drowsy warmth, and the delicious odour of wild thyme. Behind, the fosse sinks and the rampart rises high and steep—two butterflies are wheeling in uncertain flight over the summit. It is only necessary to raise the head a little way, and the cod breeze refreshes the cheek—cool at this height, while the plains beneath glow under the heat."

This, too, from *The Life of the Fields*:—

> "Green rushes, long and thick, standing up above the edge of the ditch, told the hour of the year, as distinctly as the shadow on the dial the hour of the day. Green and thick and sappy to the touch, they felt like summer, soft and elastic, as if full of life, mere rushes though they were. On the fingers they left a green scent; rushes have a separate scent of green, so, too, have ferns very different to that of

grass or leaves. Rising from brown sheaths, the tall stems, enlarged a little in the middle like classical columns, and heavy with their sap and freshness, leaned against the hawthorn sprays. From the earth they had drawn its moisture, and made the ditch dry; some of the sweetness of the air had entered into their fibres, and the rushes—the common rushes—were full of beautiful summer."

Jefferies' writings are studies in tactile sensation. This is what brings him into affinity with Keats, and this is what differentiates him from Thoreau, with whom he had much in common. Of both Jefferies and Thoreau it might be said what Emerson said of his friend, that they "saw as with a microscope, heard as with an ear-trumpet." As lovers of the open air and of the life of the open air, every sense was preternaturally quickened. But though both observed acutely, Jefferies alone felt acutely.

"To me," he says, "colour is a sort of food; every spot of colour is a drop of wine to the spirit."

It took many years for him to realize where exactly his strength as a writer lay. In early and later life he again and again essayed the novel form, but, superior as were his later fictions—*Amaryllis at the Fair*, for instance, to such crude stuff as *The Scarlet Shawl*—it is as a prose Nature poet that he will be remembered.

He knew and loved the Earth; the atmosphere of the country brought into play all the faculties of his nature. Lacking in social gifts, reserved and shy to an extreme, he neither knew much about men and women, nor cared to know much. With a few exceptions—for the most part studies of his own kith and kin—the personages of his stories are shadow people; less vital realities than the trees, the flowers, the birds, of whom he has to speak.

But where he writes of what he has felt, what he has realized, then, like every fine artist, he transmits his enthusiasm to others. Sometimes, maybe, he is so full of his subject, so engrossed with the wonders of the Earth, that the words come forth in a torrent, impetuous, overwhelming. He writes like a man beside himself with sheer joy. *The Life of the Fields* gives more than physical pleasure, more than an imaginative delight, it is a religion—the old religion of Paganism. He has, as Sir Walter Besant truly said, "communed so much with Nature, that he is intoxicated with her fulness and her beauty. He lies upon the turf, and feels the embrace of the great round world." [147]

Even apart from fiction, his earlier work varied greatly in quality. With the publication of *The Game-keeper at Home*, it was clear that a new force had entered English literature. A man of temperamental sympathies with men like Borrow and Thoreau, nevertheless with a power and individuality of his own. But if increasing years brought comparative recognition, they brought also fresh physical infirmities. The last few years of his life were one prolonged agony, and yet his finest work was done in them, and that splendid prose-poem, "The Pageant of Summer," was dictated in the direst possible pain. As the physical frame grew weaker the passion for the Earth grew in intensity; and in his writing there is all that desperate longing for the great healing forces of Nature, that ecstasy in the glorious freedom of the open air, characteristic of the sick man.

At its best Jefferies' style is rich in sensuous charm, and remarkable no less for its eloquence of thought than for its wealth of observation.

III

One characteristic of his art is of especial interest; I mean the mystical quality which he imparts to certain of his descriptions of Nature. The power of mystic suggestion is a rare one; even poets like Keats and Shelley could not always command it successfully—and perhaps Blake, Coleridge, and Rossetti alone of our poets possessed it in the highest degree. It is comparatively an easy matter to deal with the mysticism of the night. The possibilities of darkness readily impress the imagination. But the mysticism of the sunlight—the mysticism not of strange shapes, but of familiar things of every day, this, though felt by many, is the most difficult thing in the world to suggest in words.

The "visions" of Jefferies, his moods of emotional exaltation, recall not only the opium dream of De Quincey, but the ecstasies of the old Mystics. The theological colouring is not present, but there is the same sharpened condition of the senses, the same spiritual hunger for a fuller life, the same sense of physical detachment from the body.

In that fascinating volume of autobiography *The Story of my Heart*, Jefferies gives many remarkable instances of these visions. Here is one:—

> "I looked at the hills, at the dewy grass, and then up through the elm branches to the sky. In a moment all that was behind me—the house, the people, the sound—seemed to disappear and to leave me alone. Involuntarily I drew a long breath, then I breathed slowly. My thought, or inner conscience, went up through the illumined sky, and I was lost in a moment of exaltation. This lasted only a very short time, only a part of a second, and while it lasted there was no formulated wish. I was absorbed. I drank the beauty of the morning. I was exalted."

One is reminded of Tennyson's verses:—

> "Moreover, something is or seems,
> That touches me with mystic gleams,
> Like glimpses of forgotten dreams—
>
> "Of something felt, like something here;
> Of something done, I know not where;
> Such as no knowledge may declare." [149]

"Ah!" says the medical man, with a wise shake of the head, "this mental condition is a common enough phenomenon, though only on rare occasions does it express itself in literature. It is simple hysteria."

The transcendentalist who has regarded this state of mind as a spiritual revelation, and looked upon its possessor as one endowed with special powers of intuition, is indignant with this physiological explanation. He is more indignant when the medical man proceeds to explain the ecstatic trances of saints, those whom one may call professional mystics. "Brutal materialism," says the transcendentalist.

Now although hysteria is commonly regarded as a foolish exhibition of weakness on the part of some excitable men and women, there is absolutely no scientific reason why any stigma should attach to this phenomenon. Nor is there any reason why the explanation should be considered as derogatory and necessarily connected with a materialistic view of the Universe.

For what is hysteria? It is an abnormal condition of the nervous system giving rise to certain physiological and psychical manifestations. With the physiological ones we are not concerned, but the psychical manifestation should be of the greatest interest to all students of literature who are also presumably students of life. The artistic temperament is always associated with a measure of nervous instability. And where there is nervous instability there will always be a tendency to hysteria. This tendency may be kept in check by other faculties. But it is latent—ready to manifest itself in certain conditions of health or under special stress of excitement. It does not follow that every hysterical person has the artistic temperament; for nervous instability may be the outcome of nervous disease, epilepsy, insanity, or even simple neuroticism in the parents. But so powerful is the influence of the imagination over the body, that the vivid imagination connoted by the artistic temperament controls the nervous system, and when it reaches a certain intensity expresses itself in some abnormal way. And it is the abnormal psychical condition that is of so much significance in literature and philosophy.

This psychical condition is far commoner in the East than in the West. Indeed in India, training in mystical insight goes by the name of Yoga. [151a] The passive, contemplative temperament of the Oriental favours this ecstatic condition.

> "The science of the Sufis," says a Persian philosopher of the eleventh century, [151b] "aims at detaching the heart from all that is not God, and at giving to it for sole occupation the meditation of the divine being. . . . Just as the understanding is a stage of human life in which an eye opens to discuss various intellectual objects uncomprehended by sensation; just so in the prophetic the sight is illumined by a light which uncovers hidden things and objects which the intellect fails to reach. The chief properties of prophetism are perceptible only during the transport by those who embrace the Sufi life. The prophet is endowed with

qualities to which you possess nothing analogous, and which consequently you cannot possibly understand. How should you know their true nature?—what one can comprehend? But the transport which one attains by the method of the Sufis is like an immediate perception, as if one touched the objects with one's hand."

It is worthy of note how that every ecstatic condition is marked by the same characteristics; and in the confession of Jefferies, the admissions of Tennyson, and in the utterance of religious mystics of every kind, two factors detach themselves. The vision or state of mind is one of expectant wonder. Something that cannot be communicated in words thrills the entire being. That is one characteristic. The other is that this exaltation, this revelation to the senses, is one that appeals wholly to sensation. It can be felt; it cannot be apprehended by any intellectual formulæ. It can never be reduced to logical shape. And the reference to "touch" in the quotation just made will remind the reader of the important part played by the tactile sense in Jefferies' æsthetic appreciations.

We are not concerned here with any of the philosophical speculations involved in these "trance conditions." All that concerns us is the remarkable literature that has resulted from this well-ascertained psychical condition. How far the condition is the outcome of forces beyond our immediate ken which compel recognition from certain imaginative minds, how far it is a question of physical disturbance; or, in other words, how far these visions are objective realities, how far subjective, are questions that he beyond the scope of the present paper. One thing, however, is indisputable; they have exercised a great fascination over men of sensitive, nervous temperaments, and are often remarkable for the wider significance they have given to our ideals of beauty.

The fact that mysticism may arise out of morbid conditions of health does not justify us, I think, in looking upon it with Max Nordau as "the fruit of a degenerate brain." Such a criticism is at one with the linking of genius with insanity—an argument already broached in the paper dealing with Hazlitt.

Professor William James—who certainly holds no brief for the mystic—makes the interesting suggestion that "these mystical flights are inroads from the subconscious life of the cerebral activity, correlative to which we as yet know nothing." [153a]

> "As a rule," he says elsewhere, "mystical states merely add a super-sensuous meaning to the ordinary outward data of consciousness. They are excitements like the emotions of love or ambition, gifts to our spirit by means of which facts already objectively before us fall into a new expressiveness,

and make a new connection with our active life. They do not contradict these facts as such, or deny anything that our senses have immediately seized."

The connection between mysticism and hysteria, and the psychological importance of hysteria, merits the fullest consideration in dealing with the writings of these literary Vagabonds. Stevenson's mysticism is more speculative than that of Jefferies; the intellectual life played a greater share in his case, but it is none the less marked; and quite apart from, perhaps even transcending, their literary interest is the psychological significance of stories like *Markheim* and *The Strange Case of Dr. Jekyll and Mr. Hyde*.

A medical friend of Jefferies, Dr. Samuel Jones, [153b] has said, when speaking of his "ecstasies": "His is not the baneful, sensuous De Quincey opium-deliriation; he felt a purer delight than that which inspired the visions of Kubla Khan; he saw 'no damsel with a dulcimer,' but thrilled with yearning unspeakable for the 'fuller soul,' and felt in every trembling fibre of his frame the consciousness of incarnate immortality."

This attempt to exalt Jefferies at the expense of De Quincey and Coleridge seems to me unfortunate. Enough has been said already in the remarks on De Quincey to show that the dreams of De Quincey were no mere opium dreams. De Quincey was a born dreamer, and from his earliest days had visions and ecstatic moods. The opium which he took (primarily at any rate to relieve pain, not, as Dr. Jones suggests, to excite sensuous imagery) undoubtedly intensified the dream faculty, but it did not produce it.

I confess that I do not know quite what the Doctor means by preferring the "purer delight" of the Jefferies exaltation to the vision that produced *Kubla Khan*. If he implies that opium provoked the one and that "the pure breath of Nature" (to use his own phrase) inspired the other, and that the latter consequently is the purer delight, then I cannot follow his reasoning.

A vision is not the less "pure" because it has been occasioned by a drug. One of the sublimest spiritual experiences that ever happened to a man came to John Addington Symonds after a dose of chloroform. Nitrous oxide, ether, Indian hemp, opium, these things have been the means of arousing the most wonderful states of ecstatic feeling.

Then why should *Kubla Khan* be rated as a less "pure" delight than one of the experiences retailed in *The Story of my Heart*? Is our imagination so restricted that it cannot enjoy both the subtleties of Coleridge and the fuller muse of Jefferies?

The healing power of Nature has never found happier expression than in *The Story of my Heart*. In words of simple eloquence he tells us how he cured the weariness and bitterness of spirit by a journey to the seashore.

"The inner nature was faint, all was dry and tasteless; I was weary for the pure fresh springs of thought. Some instinctive feeling uncontrollable drove me to the sea. . . . Then alone I went down to the sea. I stood where the foam came to my feet, and looked out over the sunlit waters. The great earth bearing the richness of the harvest, and its hills golden with corn, was at my back; its strength and firmness under me. The great sun shone above, the wide sea was before me. The wind came sweet and strong from the waves. The life of the earth and the sea, the glow of the sun filled me; I touched the surge with my hand, I lifted my face to the sun, I opened my lips to the wind. I prayed aloud in the roar of the waves—my soul was strong as the sea, and prayed with the sea's might. Give me fulness of life like to the sea and the sun, and to the earth and the air; give me fulness of physical life, mind equal and beyond their fulness; give me a greatness and perfection of soul higher than all things; give me my inexpressible desire which swells in me like a tide—give it to me with all the force of the sea."

Those who know Jefferies only by his quieter passages of leisurely observation are surprised when they find such a swirl of passionate longing in his autobiography.

IV

The points of affinity between Thoreau and Jefferies are sufficiently obvious; and yet no two writers who have loved the Earth, and found their greatest happiness in the life of the woods and fields, as did these two men, have expressed this feeling so variously. Thoreau, quiet, passive, self-contained, has seized upon the large tranquillity of Nature, the coolness and calm, "the central piece subsisting at the heart of endless agitation." Interspersed with his freshly observed comments on the myriad life about him are moral reflections, shrewd criticism of men and things, quaint and curious illustrations from his scholarly knowledge. But although he may not always talk of the Earth, there is the flavour of the Earth, the sweetness and naturalness of the Earth, about his finest utterances.

Jefferies, feverish, excitable, passionate, alive to the glorious plenitude of the Earth, has seized upon the exceeding beauty, and the healing beauty of natural things. No scholar like Thoreau, he brings no system of thought, as did the American, for Nature to put into shape. Outside of Nature all is arid and profitless to him. He comes to her with empty hands, and seeks for what she may give him. To Thoreau the Earth was a kind and gracious sister; to Jefferies an all-sufficing mistress.

The reader who passes from Thoreau to Jefferies need have no fear that he will be wearied with the same point of view. On the contrary, he will realize with pleasure how differently two genuine lovers of the Earth can express their affection.

In Jefferies' song of praise, his song of desire—praise and desire alternate continually in his writings—there are two aspects of the Earth upon which he dwells continually—the exceeding beauty of the Earth, and the exceeding plenitude of the Earth. Apostrophes to the beauty have been quoted already; let this serve as an illustration of the other aspect:—

> "Everything," [157a] he exclaims, "on a scale of splendid waste. Such noble broadcast, open-armed waste is delicious to behold. Never was there such a lying proverb as 'Enough is as good as a feast.' [157b] Give me the feast; give me squandered millions of seeds, luxurious carpets of petals, green mountains of oak leaves. The greater the waste the greater the enjoyment—the nearer the approach to real life. Casuistry is of no avail; the fact is obvious; Nature flings treasures abroad, puffs them with open lips along on every breeze; piles up lavish layers of them in the free, open air, packs countless numbers together in the needles of a fir tree. Prodigality and superfluity are stamped on everything she does."

This is no chance passage, no casual thought. Again and again Jefferies returns to the richness and plenty of the Earth. And his style, suiting itself to the man's temperament, is rich and overflowing, splendidly diffuse, riotously exulting, until at times there is the very incoherence of passion about it.

Thus, in looking at the man's artistic work, its form of expression, its characteristic notes, something of the man's way of thinking has impressed itself upon us.

V

It may be well to gather up the scattered impressions, and to look at the thought that underlies his fervid utterances. Beginning as merely an interested observer of Nature, his attitude becomes more enthusiastic, as knowledge grows of her ways, and what began in observation ends in aspiration. The old cry, "Return to Nature," started by Rousseau, caught by the poets of the "Romantic Revival" in England, and echoed by the essayists of New England, fell into silence about the middle of last century. It had inspired a splendid group of Nature poets; and for a time it was felt some new gospel was needed. Scientific and philosophical problems took possession of men's minds; the intellectual and emotional life of the nation centred more and more round the life of the city. For a time this was, perhaps, inevitable. For a time Nature regarded through the eyes of fresh scientific thought had lost her charm. Even the poets who once had been content to worship, now began to criticize. Tennyson qualified his homage with reproachings. Arnold carried his books of philosophy into her presence. But at last men tired of this questioning attitude. America produced a Whitman; and in England William Morris and Richard Jefferies—among others—cried out for a simpler, freer, more childlike attitude.

"All things seem possible," declared Jefferies, "in the open air." To live according to Nature was, he assured his countrymen, no poet's fancy, but a creed of life. He spoke from his own experience; life in the open, tasting the wild sweetness of the Earth, had brought him his deepest happiness; and he cried aloud in his exultation, bidding others do likewise. "If you wish your children," says he, "to think deep things, to know the holiest emotions, take them to the woods and hills, and give them the freedom of the meadows." On the futility of bookish learning, the ugliness and sordidness of town life, he is always discoursing. His themes were not fresh ones; every reformer, every prophet of the age had preached from the same text. And none had put the case for Nature more forcibly than Wordsworth when he lamented—

"The world is too much with us."

But the plea for saner ways of living cannot be urged too often, and if Jefferies in his enthusiasm exaggerates the other side of the picture, pins his faith over much on solitudes and in self-communion, too little on the gregarious instincts of humankind, yet no reformer can make any impression on his fellows save by a splendid one-sidedness.

The defect of his Nature creed which calls for the most serious criticism is not the personal isolation on which he seems to insist. We herd together so much—some unhappily by necessity, some by choice, that it would be a refreshing thing, and a wholesome thing, for most of us to be alone, more often face to face with the primal forces of Nature.

The serious defect in his thought seems to me to lie in his attitude towards the animal creation. It is summed up in his remark: "There is nothing human in any living Animal. All Nature, the Universe as far as we see, is anti- or ultra-human outside, and has no concern with man." In this statement he shows how entirely he has failed to grasp the secret of the compelling power of the Earth—a secret into which Thoreau entered so fully.

Why should the elemental forces of Nature appeal so strongly to us? Why does the dweller in the open air feel that an unseen bond of sympathy binds him to the lowest forms of sentient life? Why is a St. Francis tender towards animals? Why does a Thoreau take a joy in the company of the birds, the squirrels, and feel a sense of companionship in the very flowers? Nay, more: what is it that gives a Jefferies this sense of communion? why, if the Earth has no "concern with man," should it soothe with its benison, and fire his being with such ecstatic rapture? If this doctrine of a Universal Brotherhood is a sentimental figment, the foundation is swept away at once of Jefferies' Nature creed. His sense of happiness, his delight in the Earth, may no doubt afford him consolation, but it is an irrational comfort, an agreeable delusion.

And yet no one can read a book of Jefferies without realizing that here is no sickly fancy—however sickness may have imparted a hectic colouring here and there—but that the instinct of the Artist is more reliable than the theory of the Thinker. Undoubtedly his Nature creed is less comprehensive than Thoreau's. Jefferies regarded many animals as "good sport"; Thoreau as good friends. "Hares," he says, "are almost formed on purpose to be good sport." The remark speaks volumes. A man who could say that has but a poor philosophic defence to offer for his rapt communion with Nature.

How can you have communion with something "anti- or ultra-human"? The large utterance, "All things seem possible in the open air" dwindles down rather meanly when the speaker looks at animals from the sportsman's point of view. Against his want of sympathy with the lower forms of creation one must put his warm-hearted plea for the agricultural poor. In his youth there was a certain harsh intolerance about his attitude towards his fellows, but he made ample amends in *Hodge and his Master*, still more in *The Dewy Morn*, for the narrow individualism of his earlier years.

One might criticize certain expressions as extravagant when he lashed out against the inequalities in society. But after all there is only a healthy Vagabond flavour about his fling at "modern civilization," and the genuine humanitarian feeling is very welcome. Some of his unpublished "Notes on the Labour Question" (quoted by Mr. Salt in his able study of Jefferies) are worthy of Ruskin. This, for instance, is vigorously put:—

> "'But they are paid to do it,' says Comfortable Respectability (which hates anything in the shape of a 'question,' glad to slur it over somehow). They are paid to do it. Go down into the pit yourself, Comfortable Respectability, and try it, as I have done, just one hour of a summer's day, then you will know the preciousness of a vulgar pot of beer! Three and sixpence a day is the price of these brawny muscles, the price of the rascally sherry you parade before your guests in

such pseudo-generous profusion. One guinea a week—that is one stall at the Opera. But why do they do it? Because Hunger and Thirst drive them. These are the fearful scourges, the whips worse than the knout, which lie at the back of Capital, and give it its power. Do you suppose these human beings, with minds, and souls, and feelings, would not otherwise repose on the sweet sward, and hearken to the song-birds as you may do on your lawn at Cedar Villa?"

Really the passage might have come out of *Fors Clavigera*; it is Ruskinian not only in sentiment, but in turn of expression. Ruskin impressed Jefferies very considerably, one would gather, and did much to open up his mind and broaden his sympathies. Making allowance for certain inconsistencies of mood, hope for and faith in the future, and weary scepticism, there is a fine stoicism about the philosophy of Jefferies. His was not the temperament of which optimists are made. His own terrible ill-health rendered him keenly sensitive to the pain and misery of the world. His deliberate seclusion from his fellow-men—more complete in some ways than Thoreau's, though not so ostensible—threw him back upon his own thoughts, made him morbidly introspective.

Then the æsthetic Idealism which dominated him made for melancholy, as it invariably does. The Worshipper at the shrine of Beauty is always conscious that

". . . . In the very temple of Delight
Veiled Melancholy has her sovran shrine."

He realizes the tragic ineffectuality of his aspiration—

"The desire of the moth for the star,"

as Shelley expresses it, and in this line of poetry the mood finds imperishable expression.

But the melancholy that visits the Idealist—the Worshipper of Beauty—is not by any means a mood of despair. The moth may not attain the star, but it feels there is a star to be attained. In other words, an intimate sense of the beauty of the world carries within it, however faintly, however overlaid with sick longing, a secret hope that some day things will shape themselves all right.

And thus it is that every Idealist, bleak and wintry as his mood may be, is conscious of the latency of spring. Every Idealist, like the man in the immortal allegory of Bunyan, has a key in his bosom called Promise. This it is that keeps from madness. And so while Jefferies will exclaim:—

"The whole and the worst the pessimist can say is far beneath the least particle of the truth, so immense is the misery of man." He will also declare, "There lives on in me an impenetrable belief, thought burning like the sun, that there is yet something to be found, something real, something to give each separate personality sunshine and flowers in its own existence now."

It is a mistake to attach much importance to Jefferies' attempts to systematize his views on life. He lacked the power of co-ordinating his impressions, and is at his best when giving free play to the instinctive life within him. No Vagabond writer can excel him in the expression of feeling; and yet perhaps no writer is less able than he to account for, to give a rational explanation of his feelings. He is rarely satisfactory when he begins to explain. Thoreau's lines about himself seem to me peculiarly applicable to Jefferies:—

> "I am a parcel of vain strivings tied
>   By a chance bond together,
> Dangling this way and that, their links
>   Were made so loose and wide
>   Methinks
>   For milder weather.
>
> "A bunch of violets without their roots
>   And sorrel intermixed,
> Encircled by a wisp of straw
>   Once coiled about their shoots,
>   The law
>   By which I'm fixed.
>
> "Some tender buds were left upon my stem
>   In mimicry of life,
> But ah, the children will not know
>   Till Time has withered them,
>   The woe
>   With which they're rife."

Jefferies was a brave man, with a rare supply of resolution and patience. His life was one long struggle against overwhelming odds. "Three great giants," as he puts it—"disease, despair, and poverty." Not only was his physical health against him, but his very idiosyncrasies all conspired to hinder his success. His pride and reserve would not permit him to take help from his friends. He even shrank from their sympathy. His years of isolation, voluntary isolation, put him out of touch with human society. His socialistic tendencies never made him social. His was a kind of abstract humanitarianism. A man may feel tenderly, sympathize towards humanity, yet shrink from human beings. Misanthropy did not inspire him; he did not dislike his fellow-men; it was simply that they bewildered and puzzled him; he could not get on with them. So it will be seen that he had not the consolation some men take in the sympathy and co-operation of their fellows. After all, this is more a defect of temperament than a fault of character, and he had to pay the penalty. Realizing this, it is impossible to withhold admiration for the pluck and courage of the man. As a lover of Nature, and an artist in prose, he needs no encomium to-day. In his eloquent "Eulogy" Sir Walter Besant gave fitting expression to the debt of gratitude we owe this poet-naturalist—this passionate interpreter of English country life.

What Borrow achieved for the stirring life of the road, Jefferies has done for the brooding life of the fields. What Thoreau did for the woods at Maine and the waters of Merrimac, Jefferies did for the Wiltshire streams and the Sussex hedgerows. He has invested the familiar scenery of Southern England with a new glamour, a tenderer sanctity; has arrested our indifferent vision, our careless hearing, turned our languid appreciation into a comprehending affection.

Ardent, shy, impressionable, proud, stout-hearted pagan and wistful idealist; one of the most pathetic and most interesting figures in modern literature.

VII
WALT WHITMAN

"So will I sing on, fast as fancies come;
Rudely the verse being as the mood it paints."

ROBERT BROWNING.

"A man he seems of cheerful yesterdays
And confident to-morrows."

WORDSWORTH.

I

The "good gray poet" is the supreme example of the Vagabond in literature. It is quite possible for one not drawn towards the Vagabond temperament to admire Stevenson, for Stevenson was a fine artist; to take delight in the vigorous "John Bullism" of *Lavengro*; to sympathize with the natural mysticism of Jefferies; the Puritan austerity of Thoreau. In short, there are aspects in the writings of the other "Vagabonds" in this volume which command attention quite apart from the characteristics specifically belonging to the literary Vagabond.

But it is not possible to view Whitman apart from his Vagabondage. He is proud of it, glories in it, and flings it in your face. Others, whatever strain of wildness they may have had, whatever sympathies they may have felt for the rough sweetness of the earth, however unconventional their habits, accepted at any rate the recognized conventions of literature. As men, as thinkers, they were unconventional; as artists conventional. They retained at any rate the literary garments of civilized society.

Not so Whitman. He is the Orson of literature. Unconventionality he carries out to its logical conclusion, and strides stark naked among our academies of learning. A strange, uncouth, surprising figure, it is impossible to ignore him however much he may shock our susceptibilities.

Many years ago Mr. Swinburne greeted him as "a strong-winged soul with prophetic wings"; subsequently he referred to him as a "drunken apple-woman reeling in a gutter." For this right-about-face he has been upbraided by Whitman's admirers. Certainly it is unusual to find any reader starting out to bless and ending with a curse. Usually it is the precedent of Balaam that is followed. But Mr. Swinburne's mingled feelings typify the attitude of every one who approaches the poet, though few of us can express ourselves so resourcefully as the author of *Poems and Ballads*.

There may be some students who accept Whitman without demur at the outset on his own terms. All I can say is that I never heard of one. However broad-minded you may consider yourself, however catholic in your sympathies, Whitman is bound to get athwart some pet prejudice, to discover some shred of conventionality. Gaily, heedlessly, you start out to explore his writings, just as you might start on a walking tour. He is in touch with the primal forces of Nature, you hear. "So much the better," say you; "civilization has ceased to charm." "You are enamoured of wildness." Thus men talk before camping out, captivated by the picturesque and healthy possibilities, and oblivious to the inconveniences of roughing it.

But just as some amount of training is wanted before a walking tour, or a period of camping out, so is it necessary to prepare yourself for a course of Whitman. And this, not because there is any exotic mystery about Whitman, not because there are any intellectual subtleties about his work, as there are in Browning, but because he is the pioneer of a new order, and the pioneer always challenges the old order; our tastes require adjusting before they can value it properly.

There is no question about a "Return to Nature" with Whitman. He never left it. Thoreau quitted the Emersonian study to get fresh inspiration from the woods. Even Jefferies, bred up in the country, carried about with him the delicate susceptibilities of the neurotic modern. Borrow retained a firm grip-hold of many conventions of the city. But Whitman? It was no case with him of a sojourn in the woods, or a ramble on the heath. He was a spiritual native of the woods and heath; not, as some seem to think, because he was a kind of wild barbarian who loved the rough and uncouth, and could be found only in unfrequented parts, but because he was in touch with the elemental everywhere. The wildness of Whitman, the barbarian aspects of the man, have been overrated. He is wild only in so far as he is cosmic, and the greater contains the less. He loves the rough and the smooth, not merely the rough. His songs are no mere pæans of rustic solitudes; they are songs of the crowded streets, as well of the country roads; of men and women—of every type—no less than of the fields and the streams. In fact, he seeks the elemental everywhere. Thoreau found it in the Indian, Borrow in the gypsies, Whitman, with a finer comprehensiveness, finds it in the multitude. His business is to bring it to the surface, to make men and women rejoice in—not shrink from—the great primal forces of life. But he is not for moralizing—

> "I give nothing as duties,
> What others give as duties I give as loving impulses.
> (Shall I give the heart's action as a duty?)"

He has no quarrel with civilization as such. The teeming life of the town is as wonderful to him as the big solitude of the Earth. Carlyle's pleasantry about the communistic experiments of the American Transcendentalists would have no application for him. "A return to Acorns and expecting the Golden Age to arrive."

Here is no exclusive child of Nature:—

> "I tramp a perpetual journey, . . .
> My signs are a rainproof coat, good shoes, and a staff cut from the woods . . .
> I have no chair, no church, no philosophy."

People talk of Whitman as if he relied entirely on the "staff cut from the woods"; they forget his rainproof coat and good shoes. Assuredly he has no mind to cut himself adrift from the advantages of civilization.

The rainproof coat, indeed, reminds one of Borrow's green gamp, which caused such distress to his friends and raised doubts in the minds of Mr. Watts-Dunton and Dr. Hake as to whether he was a genuine child of the

open air. [173] No one would cavil at that term as applied to Whitman—yet one must not forget the "rainproof coat."

In regarding the work of Whitman there are three aspects which strike one especially. His attitude towards Art, towards Humanity, towards Life.

II

First of all, Whitman's attitude towards Art.

For the highest art two essentials are required—Sincerity and Beauty. The tendency of modern literature has been to ignore the first and to make the second all-sufficient. The efforts of the artist have been concentrated upon the workmanship, and too often he has been satisfied with a merely technical excellence.

It is a pleasant and attractive pastime, this playing with words. Grace, charm, and brilliance are within the reach of the artificer's endeavour. But a literature which is the outcome of the striving after beauty of form, without reference to the sincerity of substance, is like a posy of flowers torn away from their roots. Lacking vitality, it will speedily perish.

No writer has seen this more clearly than Whitman, and if in his vigorous allegiance to Sincerity he has seemed oblivious at times to the existence of Beauty, yet he has chosen the better part. And for this reason. Beauty will follow in the wake of Sincerity, whether sought for or no, and the writer whose one passion it is to see things as they are, and to disentangle from the transient and fleeting the great truths of life, finds that in achieving a noble sincerity he has also achieved the highest beauty.

The great utterances of the world are beautiful, because they are true. Whereas the artist who is determined to attain beauty at all costs will obtain beauty of a kind—"silver-grey, placid and perfect," as Andrea del Sarto said, but the highest beauty it will not be, for that is no mere question of manner, but a perfect blend of manner and matter.

It will no doubt be urged that, despite his sincerity, there is a good deal in Whitman that is not beautiful. And this must be frankly conceded. But this will be found only when he has failed to separate the husk from the kernel. Whitman's sincerity is never in question, but he does not always appreciate the difference between accuracy and truth, between the accidental and the essential. For instance, lines like these—

> "The six framing men, two in the middle, and two at each end, carefully bearing on their shoulders a heavy stick for a cross-beam."

or physiological detail after this fashion:—

> "Mouth, tongue, lips, teeth, roof of the mouth, jaws and the jaw hinges,
> Nose, nostrils of the nose, and the partition,
> Cheeks, temples, forehead, chin, throat, back of the neck sheer.
> Strong shoulders, manly beard, hind shoulders, and the ample size round of the chest,
> Upper arm, armpit, elbow socket, lower arms, arm sinews,

arm bones.
Wrist and wrist joints, hand, palm, knuckles, thumb,
forefinger, finger joints, finger nails, etc., etc."

The vital idea lying beneath these accumulated facts is lost sight of by the reader who has to wade through so many accurate non-essentials.

It is well, I think, to seize upon the weakness of Whitman's literary style at the outset, for it explains so much that is irritating and disconcerting.

Leaves of Grass he called his book, and the name is more significant than one at first realizes. For there is about it not only the sweetness, the freshness, the luxuriance of the grass; but its prolific rankness—the wheat and the tares grow together.

It has, I know, been urged by some of Whitman's admirers that his power as a writer does not depend upon his artistic methods or non-artistic methods, and he himself protested against his *Leaves* being judged merely as literature. And so there has been a tendency to glorify his very inadequacies, to hold him up as a poet who has defied successfully the unwritten laws of Art.

This is to do him an ill service. If Whitman's work be devoid of Art, then it possesses no durability. Literature is an art just as much as music, painting, or sculpture. And if a man, however fine, however inspiring his ideas may be, has no power to shape them—to express them in colour, in sound, in form, in words—to seize upon the essentials and use no details save as suffice to illustrate these essentials, then his work will not last. For it has no vitality.

In other words, Whitman must be judged ultimately as an artist, for Art alone endures. And on the whole he can certainly bear the test. His art was not the conventional art of his day, but art it assuredly was.

In his best utterances there are both sincerity and beauty.

Who could deny the title of artist to the man who wrote those noble verses, "On the Beach at Night"?—

"On the beach at night,
Stands a child with her father,
Watching the east, the autumn sky.

"Up through the darkness,
While ravening clouds, the burial clouds, in black masses spreading,
Lower sullen and fast athwart and down the sky,
Amid a transparent clear belt of ether yet left in the east,
Ascends large and calm the lord-star Jupiter,

> And nigh at hand, only a very little above,
> Swim the delicate sisters the Pleiades.
>
> "From the beach the child holding the hand of her father,
> Those burial clouds that lower victorious soon to devour all
> Watching, silently weeps.
>
> "Weep not, child,
> Weep not, my darling,
> With these kisses let me remove your tears,
> The ravening clouds shall not long be victorious,
> They shall not long possess the sky, they devour the stars only in apparition,
> Jupiter shall emerge, be patient, watch again another night, the Pleiades shall emerge,
> They are immortal, all those stars both silvery and golden shall shine out again,
> The great stars and the little ones shall shine out again, they endure,
> The vast immortal suns and the long-enduring pensive moons shall again shine.
>
> "Then, dearest child, mournest thou only for Jupiter?
> Considerest thou alone the burial of the stars?
>
> "Something there is,
> (With my lips soothing thee, adding I whisper,
> I give thee the first suggestion, the problem and indirection)
> Something there is more immortal even than the stars,
> (Many the burials, many the days and nights, passing away)
> Something that shall endure longer even than lustrous Jupiter,
> Longer than sun or any revolving satellite,
> Or the radiant sisters the Pleiades."

or those touching lines, "Reconciliation"?—

> "Word over all beautiful as the sky,
> Beautiful that war and all its deeds of carnage must in time be utterly lost,
> That the hands of the sisters Death and Night incessantly
> Wash again, and ever again, this soil'd world;
> For my enemy is dead, a man divine as myself is dead,
> I look where he lies white-faced and still in the coffin—
> I draw near—

> Bend down and touch lightly with my lips the white face in the coffin."

Again, take that splendid dirge in memory of President Lincoln, majestic in its music, spacious and grand in its treatment. It is too long for quotation, but the opening lines, with their suggestive beauty, and the Song to Death, may be instanced.

> "When lilacs last in the dooryard bloomed,
> And the great star early droop'd in the western sky in the night,
> I mourned, and yet shall mourn with ever-returning spring.
> Ever-returning spring, trinity sure to me you bring
> Lilac blooming perennial and drooping star in the west,
> And thought of him I love.
>
> "O powerful western fallen star!
> O shades of night—O moody, tearful night!
> O great star disappear'd—O the black murk that hides the star!
> O cruel hands that hold me powerless—O helpless soul of me!
> O harsh surrounding cloud that will not free my soul!
>
> "In the dooryard fronting an old farmhouse near the whitewash'd palings,
> Stands the lilac-bush tall-growing with heart-shaped leaves of rich green,
> With many a pointed blossom rising delicate, with the perfume strong I love.
> With every leaf a miracle—and from this bush in the dooryard,
> With delicate coloured blossoms and heart-shaped leaves of rich green,
> A sprig with its flower I break.
>
> * * * * *
>
> "Come lovely and soothing death,
> Undulate round the world, serenely arriving, arriving,
> In the day, in the night, to all, to each,
> Sooner or later delicate death.
>
> "Prais'd be the fathomless universe,
> For life and joy, and for objects and knowledge curious,

And for love, sweet love—but praise! praise! praise!
For the sure-enwinding arms of cool-enfolding death.

"Dark mother always gliding near with soft feet,
Have none chanted for thee a chant of fullest welcome?
Then I chant it for thee, I glorify thee above all,
I bring thee a song that when thou must indeed come, come unfalteringly.

* * * * *

"The night in silence under many a star,
The ocean shore and the husky whispering wave whose voice I know,
And the soul-turning to thee, O vast and well-veil'd death,
And the body gratefully nestling close to thee.

"Over the tree-tops I float thee a song,
Over the rising and sinking waves, over the myriad fields and the prairies wide,
Over the dense-pack'd cities all and the teeming wharves and ways,
I float this carol with joy, with joy to thee, O death."

This is not only Art, but great Art. So fresh in their power, so striking in their beauty, are Whitman's utterances on Death that they take their place in our memories beside the large utterances of Shakespeare, Milton, and Shelley.

It is a mistake to think that where Whitman fails in expression it is through carelessness; that he was a great poet by flashes, and that had he taken more pains he would have been greater still. We have been assured by those who knew him intimately that he took the greatest care over his work, and would wait for days until he could get what he felt to be the right word.

To the student who comes fresh to a study of Whitman it is conceivable that the rude, strong, nonchalant utterances may seem like the work of an inspired but careless and impatient artist. It is not so. It is done deliberately.

"I furnish no specimens," he says; "I shower them by exhaustless laws, fresh and modern continually, as Nature does."

He is content to be suggestive, to stir your imagination, to awaken your sympathies. And when he fails, he fails as Wordsworth did, because he lacked the power of self-criticism, lacked the faculty of humour—that saving faculty which gives discrimination, and intuitively protects the artist from confusing pathos with bathos, the grand and the grandiose. Nowhere is this more apparent than in his treatment of Sex. Frankness, outspokenness on the primal facts of life are to be welcomed in literature. All the great masters—Shakespeare, Dante, Dostoievsky, Tolstoy, have dealt openly and fearlessly with the elemental passions. There is nothing to deplore in this, and Mr. Swinburne was quite right when he contended that the domestic circle is not to be for all men and writers the outer limit of their world of work. So far from regretting that Whitman claimed right to equal freedom when speaking of the primal fact of procreation as when speaking of sunrise, sunsetting, and the primal fact of death, every clean-minded man and woman should rejoice in the poet's attitude. For he believed and gloried in the separate personalities of man and woman, claiming manhood and womanhood as the poet's province, exulting in the potentialities of a healthy sexual life. He was angry, as well he might be, with the furtive snigger which greets such matters as motherhood and fatherhood with the prurient unwholesomeness of a mind that can sigh sentimentally over the "roses and raptures of Vice" and start away shamefaced from the stark passions—stripped of all their circumlocutions. He certainly realized as few have done the truth of that fine saying of Thoreau's, that "for him to whom sex is impure there are no flowers in Nature."

But at the same time I cannot help feeling that Stevenson was right when he said that Whitman "loses our sympathy in the character of a poet by attracting too much of our attention—that of a Bull in a China Shop." [180]

His aim is right enough; it is to his method one may take objection. Not on the score of morality. Whitman's treatment of passion is not immoral; it is simply like Nature herself—unmoral. What shall we say then about his sex cycle, "Children of Adam"? Whitman, in his anxiety to speak out, freely, simply, naturally, to vindicate the sanity of coarseness, the poetry of animalism, seems to me to have bungled rather badly. There are many fine passages in his "Song of the Body Electric" and "Spontaneous Me," but much of it impresses me as bad art, and is consequently ineffectual in its aim. The subject demands a treatment at once strong and subtle—I do not mean finicking—and subtlety is a quality not vouchsafed to Whitman. Lacking it, he is often unconsciously comic where he should be gravely impressive. "A man's body is sacred, and a woman's body is sacred." True; but the sacredness is not displayed by making out a tedious inventory of the various parts of the body. Says Whitman in effect: "The sexual life is to be gloried in, not to be treated as if it were something shameful." Again true; but is there not a danger of missing the glory by discoursing noisily on the various physiological manifestations. Sex is not the more wonderful for being appraised by the big drum.

The inherent beauty and sanctity of Sex lies surely in its superb unconsciousness; it is a matter for two human beings drawn towards one another by an indefinable, world-old attraction; scream about it, caper over it, and you begin to make it ridiculous, for you make it self-conscious.

Animalism merely as a scientific fact serves naught to the poet, unless he can show also what is as undeniable as the bare fact—its poetry, its coarseness, and its mystery go together. Browning has put it in a line:—

> ". . . savage creatures seek
> Their loves in wood and plain—*and GOD renews*
> *His ancient rapture.*"

It is the "rapture" and the mystery which Whitman misses in many of his songs of Sex.

There is no need to give here any theological significance to the word "God." Let the phrase stand for the mystic poetry of animalism. Whitman has no sense of mystery.

I have another objection against "The Children of Adam." The loud, self-assertive, genial, boastful style of Whitman suits very well many of his democratic utterances, his sweeping cosmic emotions. But here it gives one the impression of a kind of showman, who with a flourishing stick is shouting out to a gaping crowd the excellences of manhood and womanhood. Deliberately he has refrained from the mood of imaginative fervour which alone could give a high seriousness to his treatment—a high seriousness which is really indispensable. And his rough, slangy, matter-of-fact comments give an atmosphere of unworthy vulgarity to his subject. Occasionally he is carried away by the sheer imaginative beauty of the subject, then note how different the effect:—

> "Have you ever loved the body of a woman,
> Have you ever loved the body of a man,
> Do you not see that these are exactly the same to all in all
> Nations and times all over the earth?"

> "If anything is sacred, the human body is sacred,
> And the glory and sweet of a man is the token of manhood untainted,
> And in man or woman a clean, strong, firm-fibred body is
> More beautiful than the most beautiful face."

If only all had been of this quality. But interspersed with lines of great force and beauty are cumbrous irrelevancies, wholly superfluous details.

William Morris has also treated the subject of Sex in a frank, open fashion. And there is in his work something of the easy, deliberate spaciousness that we find in Whitman. But Morris was an artist first and foremost, and he never misses the *poetry* of animalism; as readers of the "Earthly Paradise" and the prose romances especially know full well.

It is not then because Whitman treats love as an animal passion that I take objection to much in his "Children of Adam." There are poets enough and to spare who sing of the sentimental aspects of love. We need have no quarrel with Whitman's aim as expressed by Mr. John Burroughs: "To put in his sex poems a rank and healthy animality, and to make them as frank as the shedding of pollen by the trees, strong even to the point of offence." All we ask is for him to do so as a poet, not as a mere physiologist. And when he speaks one moment as a physiologist, next as a poet; at one time as a lover, at another as a showman, the result is not inspiring. "He could not make it pleasing," remarks Mr. Burroughs, "a sweet morsel to be rolled under the tongue; that would have been levity and sin, as in Byron and the other poets ... He would sooner be bestial than Byronic, he would sooner shock by his frankness than inflame by his suggestion." This vague linking together of "Byron and the other poets" is not easy to understand. In the first place, not one of the moderns has treated love from the same standpoint. Shelley, for instance, is transcendental, Byron elemental, Tennyson sentimental; Rossetti looks at the soul through the body, Browning regards the body through the soul. There is abundant variety in the treatment. Then, again, why Byron should be singled out especially for opprobrium I fail to see, for love is to him the fierce elemental passion it is for Whitman. As for frankness, the episode of Haidee and Don Juan does not err on the side of reticence. Nor is it pruriently suggestive. It is a splendid piece of poetic animalism. Let us be fair to Byron. His work may in places be disfigured by an unworthy cynicism; his treatment of sexual problems be marred by a shallow flippancy. But no poet had a finer appreciation of the essential poetry of animalism than he, and much of his cynicism, after all, is by way of protest against the same narrow morality at which Whitman girds. To single Byron out as a poet especially obnoxious in his treatment of love, and to condemn him so sweepingly, seems to me scarcely defensible. To extol unreservedly the rankness and coarseness of "The Children of Adam," and to have no word of commendation, say, for so noble a piece of naturalism as the story of Haidee, seems to me lacking in fairness. Besides, it suggests that the *only* treatment in literature of the sexual life is a coarse, unpleasing treatment, which I do not suppose Mr. Burroughs really holds. Whitman has vindicated, and vindicated finely, the inherent truth and beauty of animalism. But so has William Morris, so has Dante Gabriel Rossetti, so has poor flouted Byron. And I will go further, and say that these other poets have succeeded often where Whitman has failed; they have shown the beauty and cosmic significance, when Whitman has been merely cataloguing the stark facts.

It may be objected, of course, that Whitman does not aim in his sex poems at imaginative beauty, that he aims at sanity and wholesomeness; that what he speaks—however rank—makes for healthy living. May be; I am not concerned to deny it. What I do deny is the implication that the wholesomeness of a fact is sufficient justification for its treatment in literature. There are a good many disagreeable things that are wholesome enough, there are many functions of the body that are entirely healthy. But one does not want them enshrined in Art.

To attack Whitman on the score of morality is unjustifiable; his sex poems are simply unmoral. But had he flouted his art less flagrantly in them they would have been infinitely more powerful and convincing, and given the Philistines less opportunity for blaspheming.

I have dwelt at this length upon Whitman's treatment of Sex largely because it illustrates his strength and weakness as a literary artist. In some of his poems—those dealing with Democracy, for instance—we have Whitman at his best. In others, certainly a small proportion, we get sheer, unillumined doggerel. In his sex poems there are great and fine ideas, moments of inspiration, flashes of beauty, combined with much that is trivial and tiresome.

But this I think is the inevitable outcome of his style. The style, like the man, is large, broad, sweeping, tolerant; the sense of "mass and multitude" is remarkable; he aims at big effects, and the quality of vastness in his writings struck John Addington Symonds as his most remarkable characteristic. [186] This vast, rolling, processional style is splendidly adapted for dealing with the elemental aspects of life, with the vital problems of humanity. He sees everything in bulk. His range of vision is cosmic. The very titles are suggestive of his point of view—"A Song of the Rolling Earth," "A Song of the Open Road," "A Song for Occupation," "Gods." There are no detailed effects, no delicate points of light and shade in his writings, but huge panoramic effects. It is a great style, it is an impressive style, but it is obviously not a plastic style, nor a versatile style. Its very merits necessarily carry with them corresponding defects. The massiveness sometimes proves mere unwieldiness, the virile strength tends to coarseness, the eye fixed on certain broad distant effects misses the delicate by-play of colour and movement in the foreground. The persistent unconventionality of metre and rhythm becomes in time a mannerism as pronounced as the mannerism of Tennyson and Swinburne.

I do not urge these things in disparagement of Whitman. No man can take up a certain line wholeheartedly and uncompromisingly without incurring the disabilities attaching to all who concentrate on one great issue.

And if sometimes he is ineffectual, if on occasion he is merely strident in place of authoritative, how often do his utterances carry with them a superb force and a conviction which compel us to recognize the sagacious genius of the man.

III

Indeed, it is when we examine Whitman's attitude towards Humanity that we realize best his strength and courage. For it is here that his qualities find their fittest artistic expression. Nothing in Whitman's view is common or unclean. All things in the Universe, rightly considered, are sweet and good. Carrying this view into social politics, Whitman declares for absolute social equality. And this is done in no doctrinaire spirit, but because of Whitman's absolute faith and trust in man and woman—not the man and woman overridden by the artifices of convention, but the "powerful uneducated person." Whitman finds his ideal not in Society (with a capital S), but in artisans and mechanics. He took to his heart the mean, the vulgar, the coarse, not idealizing their weaknesses, but imbuing them with his own strength and vigour.

> "I am enamoured of growth out of doors,
> Of men that live among cattle, or taste of the ocean or woods,
> Of the builder and steerers of ships, and the wielders of axes, and
> The drivers of horses.
> I can eat and sleep with them week in week out."

Such are his comrades. And well he knows them. For many years of his life he was roving through country and city, coming into daily contact with the men and women about whom he has sung. Walt Whitman—farm boy, school teacher, printer, editor, traveller, mechanic, nurse in the army hospital, Government clerk. Truly our poet has graduated as few have done in the school of Life. No writer of our age has better claims to be considered the Poet of Democracy.

But he was no sentimentalist. More tolerant and passive in disposition than Victor Hugo, he had the same far-seeing vision when dealing with the people. He recognized their capacity for good, their unconquerable faith, their aspirations, their fine instincts; but he recognized also their brutality and fierceness. He would have agreed with Spencer's significant words: "There is no alchemy by which you can get golden conduct out of leaden instincts"; but he would have denied Spencer's implication that leaden instincts ruled the Democracy. And he was right. There is more real knowledge of men and women in *Leaves of Grass* and *Les Miserables* than in all the volumes of the Synthetic Philosophy. Thus Whitman announces his theme:—

"Of Life immense in passion, pulse, and power,
Cheerful, for freest action formed under the laws divine.
The modern man I sing."

"Whitman," wrote the late Mr. William Clarke, in his stimulating study of the Poet, [188] "sings of the Modern Man as workman, friend, citizen, brother, comrade, as pioneer of a new social order, as both material and spiritual, final and most subtle, compound of spirit and nature, firmly planted on this rolling earth, and yet 'moving about in worlds not realized.' As representative democratic bard Whitman exhibits complete freedom from unconventionality, a very deep human love for all, faith in the rationality of the world, courage, energy, and the instincts of solidarity."

In the introductory essay to this volume some remarks were made about the affections of the literary Vagabond in general and of Whitman in particular, which call now for an ampler treatment, especially as on this point I find myself, apparently, at issue with so many able and discerning critics of Whitman. I say apparently because a consideration of the subject may show that the difference, though real, is not so fundamental as it appears to be.

That Whitman entertained a genuine affection for men and women is, of course, too obvious to be gainsaid. His noble work in the hospitals, his tenderness towards criminals and outcasts—made known to us through the testimony of friends—show him to be a man of comprehensive sympathies. No man of a chill and calculating nature could have written as he did, and, although his writings are not free of affectation, the strenuous, fundamental sincerity of the man impresses every line.

But was it, to quote William Clarke, "a *very deep* human love"? This seems to me a point of psychological interest. A man may exhibit kindliness and tenderness towards his fellow-creatures without showing any deep personal attachment. In fact, the wider a man's sympathies are the less room is there for any strong individual feeling. His friend, Mr. Donaldson, has told us that he never remembers Whitman shedding a tear of grief over the death of any friend. Tears of joy he shed often; but no tear of sorrow, of personal regret. It is true that Mr. Donaldson draws no particular inference from this fact. It seems to me highly significant. The absence of intense emotion is no argument truly for insensibility; but to a man of large, sweeping sympathies such as Whitman the loss of a particular friend did not strike home as it would do in men of subtler temperaments.

Cosmic emotions leave no room for those special manifestations of concentrated feeling in individual instances which men with a narrower range of sympathies frequently show.

For in denying that Whitman was a man capable of "a very deep human love," no moral censure is implied. If not deep, it was certainly comprehensive; and rarely, if ever, do the two qualities coexist. Depth of feeling is not to be found in men of the tolerant, passive type; it is the intolerant, comparatively narrow-minded man who loves deeply; the man of few friends, not the man who takes the whole human race to his heart in one colossal embrace. Narrowness may exist, of course, without intensity. But intensity of temperament always carries with it a certain forceful narrowness. Such a man, strongly idiosyncratic, with his sympathies running in a special groove, is capable of one or two affections that absorb his entire nature. Those whom he cares for are so subtly bound up with the peculiarities of his temperament that they become a part of his very life. And if they go, so interwoven are their personalities with the fibres of his being, that part of his life goes with them. To such the death of an intimate friend is a blow that shatters them beyond recovery. Courage and endurance, indeed, they may show, and the undiscerning may never note how fell the blow has been. But though the healing finger of Time will assuage the wound, the scars they will carry to their dying day.

As a rule, such men, lovable as they may be to the few, are not of the stuff of which social reformers are made. They feel too keenly, too sensitively, are guided too much by individual temperamental preferences. It is of no use for any man who has to deal with coarse-grained humanity, with all sorts and conditions of men, to be fastidious in his tastes. A certain bluntness, a certain rude hardiness, a certain evenness of disposition is absolutely necessary. We are told of Whitman by one of his most ardent admirers that his life was "a pleased, uninterested saunter through the world—no hurry, no fever, no strife, hence no bitterness, no depression, no wasted energies . . . in all his tastes and attractions always aiming to live thoroughly in the free nonchalant spirit of the day."

Yes; this is the type of man wanted as a social pioneer, as a poet of the people. A man who felt more acutely, for whom the world was far too terrible a place for sauntering, would be quite unfitted for Whitman's task. It was essential that he should have lacked deep individual affection. Something had to be sacrificed for the work he had before him, and we need not lament that he had no predilection for those intimate personal ties that mean so much to some.

A man who has to speak a word of cheer to so many can ill afford to linger with the few. He is not even concerned to convert you to his way of thinking. He throws out a hint, a suggestion, the rest you must do for yourself.

"I am a man who, sauntering along without fully stopping, turns a casual look upon you, and then averts his face. Leaving you to prove and define it. Expecting the main things from you."

Nowhere are Whitman's qualities more admirably shown than in his attitude towards the average human being. As a rule the ordinary man is not a person whom the Poet delights to honour. He is concerned with the exceptional, the extraordinary type. Whitman's attitude then is of special interest.

> "I will leave all and come and make the hymns of you;
> None has understood you, but I understand you;
> None has done justice to you—you have not done justice
> to yourself.
> None but has found you imperfect; I only find no
> imperfection in you.
> None but would subordinate you; I only am he who will
> never consent to subordinate you."
>
> * * * * *
>
> "Painters have painted their swarming groups, and the
> centre figure of all;
> From the head of the centre figure, spreading a nimbus of
> gold-coloured light.
> But I paint myriads of heads, but paint no head without its
> nimbus of gold-coloured light.
> From My hand, from the brain of every man and woman
> it streams effulgently flowing for ever.
> O! I could sing such grandeurs and glories about you!
> You have not known what you are; you have slumbered
> upon yourself all your time. . . ."

And so on, in a vein of courageous cheer, spoken with the big, obtrusive, genial egotism that always meets us in Whitman's writings. Whitman's egotism proves very exasperating to some readers, but I do not think it should trouble us much. After all it is the egotism of a simple, natural, sincere nature; there is no self-satisfied smirk about it, no arrogance. He is conscious of his powers, and is quite frank in letting you know this. Perhaps his boisterous delight in his own prowess may jar occasionally on the nerves; but how much better than the affected humility of some writers. And the more you study his writings the less does this egotism affect even the susceptible. Your ears get attuned to the pitch of the voice, you realize that the big drum is beaten with a purpose. For it must be remembered that it is an egotism entirely emptied of condescension. He is vain certainly, but mainly because he glories in the common heritage, because he feels he is one of the common people. He is proud assuredly, but it is pride that exults in traits that he shares in common with the artist, the soldier, and the sailor. He is no writer who plays down to the masses, who will prophesy fair things—like the mere demagogue—in order to win their favour. And it is a proof of his plain speaking, of his fearless candour, that for the most part the very men for whom he wrote care little for him.

Conventionality rules every class in the community. Whitman's gospel of social equality is not altogether welcome to the average man. One remembers Mr. Barrie's pleasant satire of social distinction in *The Admirable Crichton*, where the butler resents his radical master's suggestion that no real difference separates employer and employed. He thinks it quite in keeping with the eternal fitness of things that his master should assert the prerogative of "Upper Dog," and points out how that there are many social grades below stairs, and that an elaborate hierarchy separates the butler at one end from the "odds and ends" at the other.

In like manner the ordinary citizen resents Whitman's genuine democratic spirit, greatly preferring the sentimental Whiggism of Tennyson.

Whitman reminds us by his treatment of the vulgar, the ordinary, the commonplace, that he signalizes a new departure in literature. Of poets about the people there have been many, but he is the first genuine Poet *of* the People.

Art is in its essence aristocratic, it strives after selectness, eschews the trivial and the trite. There is, therefore, in literature always a tendency towards conservatism; the literary artist grows more and more fastidious in his choice of words; the cheap and vulgar must be rigorously excluded, and only those words carrying with them stately and beautiful associations are to be countenanced. Thus Classicism in Art constantly needs the freshening, broadening influence of Romanticism.

What Conservatism and Liberalism are to Politics Classicism and Romanticism are to Art. Romantic revolutions have swept over literature before the nineteenth century, and Shakespeare was the first of our great Romantics. Then with the reaction Formalism and Conservatism crept in again. But the Romantic Revival at the beginning of the nineteenth century went much further than previous ones. Out of the throes of the Industrial Revolution had been born a lusty, clamorous infant that demanded recognition—the new Demos. And it claimed not only recognition in politics, but recognition in literature. Wordsworth and Shelley essayed to speak for it with varying success; but Wordsworth was too exclusive, and Shelley—the most sympathetic of all our poets till the coming of Browning—was too ethereal in his manner. Like his own skylark, he sang to us poised midway between earth and heaven; a more emphatically flesh and blood personage was wanted.

Here and there a writer of genuine democratic feeling, like Ebenezer Elliott, voiced the aspirations of the people, but only on one side. Thomas Hood and Mrs. Browning sounded a deeper note; but the huge, clamorous populace needed a yet fuller note, a more penetrating insight, a more forceful utterance. And in America, with its seething democracy—a democracy more urgent, more insistent than our own—it found its spokesman. That it did not recognize him, and is only just beginning to do so, is not remarkable. It did not recognize him, for it had scarcely recognized itself. Only dimly did it realize its wants and aspirations. Whitman divined them; he is the Demos made articulate.

And not only did he sweep away the Conservative traditions and conventions of literature, he endeavoured to overthrow the aristocratic principle that underlies it. Selectness he would replace with simplicity. No doubt he went too far. That is of small moment. Exaggeration and over-emphasis have their place in the scheme of things. A thunderstorm may be wanted to clear the air, and if it does incidentally some slight damage to crops and trees it is of no use grumbling.

But in the main Whitman's theory of Art was very true and finely suggestive, and is certainly not the view of a man who cares for nothing but the wild and barbaric.

> "The art of Art, the glory of expression, and the sunshine of the light of letters is simplicity. Nothing is better than simplicity, nothing can make up for excess or for the lack of definiteness. To carry on the heave of impulse, and pierce intellectual depths, and give all subjects their articulations, are powers neither common nor very uncommon. But to speak in literature with the perfect rectitude and insouciance of the movements of animals and the unimpeachableness of the sentiment of trees in the woods, and grass by the woodside, is the flawless triumph of Art."

A fitting attitude for a Poet of Democracy, one likely to bring him into direct contact with the broad, variegated stream of human life.

What perhaps he did not realize so clearly is that Nature, no less than Art, exercises the selective facility, and corrects her own riotous extravagance. And thus on occasion he falls into the very indefiniteness, the very excess he deprecates.

The way in which his Art and democratic spirit correspond suggests another, though less unconventional poet of the Democracy—William Morris. The spaciousness the directness, the tolerance that characterise Whitman's work are to be found to Morris. Morris had no eclectic preferences either in Art or Nature. A wall paper, a tapestry, an epic were equally agreeable tasks; and a blade of grass delighted him as fully as a sunset. So with men. He loved many, but no one especially. Catholicity rather than intensity characterised his friendships. And, like Whitman, he could get on cheerfully enough with surprisingly unpleasant people, provided they were working for the cause in which he was interested. [197] That is the secret. Whitman and Morris loved the Cause. They looked at things in the mass, at people in the mass. This is the true democratic spirit. They had no time, nor must it be confessed any special interest—in the individual as such. What I have said about Whitman's affection being comprehensive rather than intense applies equally to Morris. Why? Because it is the way of the Democrat and the Social Reformer. To such the individual suggests a whole class, a class suggests the race. Whitman is always speaking to man as man, rarely does he touch on individual men. If he does so, it is only to pass on to some cosmic thoughts suggested by the particular instance.

Perhaps the most inspiring thing about Whitman's attitude towards humanity is his thorough understanding of the working classes, and his quick discernment of the healthy naturalism that animates them. He neither patronizes them nor idealizes them; he sees their faults, which are obvious enough; but he also sees, what is not so obvious, their fine independence of spirit, their eager thirst for improvement, for ampler knowledge, for larger opportunities, and their latent idealism.

No doubt there is more independence, greater vigour, less servility, in America than in England; but the men he especially delights in, the artisan or mechanic, represent the best of the working classes in either country.

In this respect Whitman and Tolstoy, differing in so many ways, join hands. In the "powerful uneducated person" they see the salvation of society, the renovation of its anæmic life.

IV

Whitman is no moralist, and has no formal philosophy to offer. But the modern spirit which always seeks after some "criticism of life" does not forsake even the Vagabond. He is certainly the only Vagabond, with the exception of Thoreau, who has felt himself charged with a message for his fellows. The popular tendency is to look for a "message" in all literary artists, and the result is that the art in question is knocked sometimes out of all shape in order to wrest from it some creed or ethical teaching. And as the particular message usually happens to be something that especially appeals to the seeker, the number of conflicting messages wrung from the unfortunate literary artist are somewhat disconcerting.

But in Whitman's case the task of the message hunter is quite simple. Whitman never leaves us in doubt what he believes in, and what ideas he wishes to propagate. It is of course easy—perhaps inevitable—that with a writer whose method it is to hint, suggest, indicate, rather than formulate, elaborate, codify, the student should read in more than was intended. And, after all, as George Eliot said, "The words of Genius bear a wider meaning than the thought which prompted them." But at any rate there is no mistaking the general outline of his thought, for his outlook upon life is as distinctive as Browning's, and indeed possesses many points of similarity. But in speaking of Whitman's message one thing must be borne in mind. Whitman's work must not be adjudged merely as a special blend of Altruism and Individualism. No man ever works, it has been well said [199]— not even if philanthropy be his trade—from the primary impulse to help or console other people, any more than his body performs its functions for the sake of other people. And what Professor Nettleship says of Browning might be applied with equal truth to Whitman. His work consists "not in his being a teacher, or even wanting to be one, but in his doing exactly the work he liked best and could not help doing." And Whitman's stimulating thought is not the less true for that, for it is the spontaneous expression of his personality, just as fully as a melody or picture is an expression of an artist's personality. He could no more help being a teacher than he could help breathing. And his teaching must be valued not in accordance with the philosophy of the schools, not by comparison with the ethics of the professional moralist, but as the natural and inevitable outcome of his personality and temperament.

As a panacea for social evils Whitman believes in the remedial power of comradeship in a large-hearted charity.

> "You felons on trial in courts,
> You convicts in prison cells, you sentenced assassins chained and handcuffed with iron,
> Who am I, too, that I am not on trial or in prison?
> Me ruthless and devilish as any, that my wrists are not chained
> With iron, or my ankles with iron?"

Mark the watchful impassiveness with which he gazes at the ugly side of life.

> "I sit and look out upon all the sorrows of the world, and upon all oppression and shame;
> I hear convulsive sobs from young men at anguish with themselves, remorseful after deeds done;
>
> * * * * *

> I see the workings of battle, pestilence, tyranny;
> I see martyrs and prisoners—
> I observe a famine at sea—I observe the sailors casting lots who shall be killed, to preserve the lives of the rest;
> I observe the slights and degradations cast by arrogant persons upon labourers, the poor, and upon negroes and the like;
> All these—all the meanness and agony without end, I sit and look out upon,
> See, hear, and am silent."

No one is too base, too degraded for Whitman's affection. This is no mere book sentiment with him; and many stories are told of his tenderness and charity towards the "dregs of humanity." That a man is a human being is enough for Whitman. However he may have fallen there is something in him to appeal to. He would have agreed with Browning that—

> "Beneath the veriest ash there hides a spark of soul,
> Which, quickened by Love's breath, may yet pervade the whole
> O' the grey, and free again be fire; of worth the same
> Howe'er produced, for great or little flame is flame."

Like Browning, also, Whitman fears lassitude and indifference more than the turmoil of passion. He glories in the elemental. At present he thinks we are too fearful of coarseness and rankness, lay too much stress on refinement. And so he delights in "unrefinement," glories in the woods, air-sweetness, sun-tan, brawn.

> "*So long!*
> I announce a life that shall be copious, vehement, spiritual bold,
> And I announce an did age that shall lightly and joyfully meet its translation."

Cultured conventions, of which we make so much, distress him. They tend, he argues, to enervation, to a poor imitative, self-conscious art, to an artificial, morbid life.

His curative methods were heroic; but who can say that they were not needed, or that they were mischievous?

Certainly in aiming first of all at sincerity he has attained that noble beauty which is born of strength. Nature, as he saw, was full of vital loveliness by reason of her very power. The average literary artist is always seeking for the loveliness, aiming after beauty of form, without a care whether what he is saying has the ring of sincerity and truth, whether it is in touch with the realities of Nature. And in his super-refinements he misses the beauty that flashes forth from the rough, savage songs of Whitman.

Whitman does not decry culture. But he places first the educative influence of Nature. "The best Culture," he says, "will always be that of the manly and courageous instincts and loving perception, and of self-respect."

No advocate of lawlessness he; the influence of modern sciences informs every line that he has written.

As Mr. Burroughs very justly says: "Whitman's relation to science is fundamental and vital. It is the soil under his feet. He comes into a world from which all childish fear and illusion has been expelled. He exhibits the religious and poetic faculties perfectly adjusted to a scientific, industrial, democratic age, and exhibits them more fervent and buoyant than ever before. We have gained more than we have lost. The world is anew created by science and democracy, and he pronounces it good with the joy and fervour of the old faith."

In this respect Mr. Burroughs thinks that Whitman shared with Tennyson the glory of being one of the two poets in our time who have drawn inspiration from this source. Certainly no poet of our time has made finer use as an artist of scientific facts than the late Laureate.

But Tennyson seems scarcely to have drawn inspiration from science as did Browning, if we look at the thought underlying the verse. On the whole scientific discoveries depressed rather than cheered him, whereas from *Paracelsus* onwards Browning accepts courageously all the results of modern science, and, as in the case of Whitman, it enlarged his moral and spiritual horizon.

But he was not a philosopher as Browning was; indeed, there is less of the philosopher about Whitman than about any poet of our age. His method is quite opposed to the philosophic. It is instinctive, suggestive, and as full of contradictions as Nature herself. You can no more extract a philosophy from his sweeping utterances than you can from a tramp over the hills.

But, like a tramp over the hills, Whitman fits every reader who accompanies him for a stronger and more courageous outlook. It is not easy to say with Whitman as in the case of many writers: "This line quickened my imagination, that passage unravelled my perplexities." It is the general effect of his writings that exercises such a remarkable tonic influence. Perhaps he has never indicated this cumulative power more happily than in the lines that conclude his "Song of Myself."

> "You will hardly know who I am, or what I mean,
> But I shall be good health to you nevertheless,
> And filter and fibre your blood.

> "Failing to fetch me at first keep encouraged.
> Missing me one place search another,
> I stop somewhere waiting for you."

Yes; that is Whitman's secret—"Good health." To speak of him as did his biographer, Dr. Bucke, as "perhaps the most advanced nature the world has yet produced," to rank him, as some have done, with the world's greatest moral teachers, beside Jesus and Socrates, seems to me the language of hysterical extravagant. Nay, more, it misses surely the special significant of his genius.

In his religious thought, his artistic feelings, his affections, there is breadth of sympathy, sanity of outlook, but an entire absence of intensity, of depth.

We shall scan his pages vainly for the profound aspiration, the subtle spiritual insight of our greatest religious teachers. In his indifference to form, his insensibility to the noblest music, we shall realize his artistic limitations.

Despite his genial comradeship, the more intimate, the more delicate experiences of friendship are not to be found in his company. Delicacy, light and shade, subtlety, intensity, for these qualities you must not seek Whitman. But that is no reason for neglecting him. The Modern and Ancient world are rich in these other qualities, and the special need of the present day is not intensity so much as sanity, not subtlety so much as breadth.

In one of his clever phrases Mr. Havelock Ellis has described Whitman "as a kind of Titanic Undine." [204] Perhaps it is a good thing for us that he never "found his soul." In an age of morbid self-introspection there is something refreshing in an utterance like this, where he praises the animals because—

> "They do not screech and whine about their condition,
> They do not lie awake in the dark and weep for their sins,
> They do not make me sick discussing their duty to GOD."

In a feverish, restless age it is well to feel the presence of that large, passive, tolerant figure. There is healing in the cool, firm touch of his hand; healing in the careless, easy self-confidence of his utterance. He has spoken to us of "the amplitude of the earth, and the coarseness and sexuality of the earth, and the great charity of the earth." And he has done this with the rough outspokenness of the elements, with the splendid audacity of Nature herself. Brawn, sun-tan, air-sweetness are things well worth the having, for they mean good health. That is why we welcome the big, genial sanity of Walt Whitman, for he has about him the rankness and sweetness of the Earth.

BIBLIOGRAPHICAL NOTES

(Some of the most noteworthy books and articles dealing with the authors discussed in this volume are indicated below.)

WILLIAM HAZLITT (1778–1830).

Memoirs, by William Carew Hazlitt. *Four Generations of a Literary Family*, by W. C. Hazlitt (1897). *William Hazlitt*, by Augustine Birrell. *William Hazlitt*, by Alexander Ireland (Frederick Warne & Co., 1889).

THOMAS DE QUINCEY (1785–1859).

De Quincey, by David Masson (Macmillan & Co.). *De Quincey and his Friends*, by James Hogg (1895). *De Quincey*, by H. S. Salt ("Bell's Miniature Series of Great Writers").

GEORGE BORROW (1803–81).

Life and Letters (2 vols.), by Dr. Knapp. Introductions to *Lavengro* (Frederick Warne & Co.), *The Romany Rye* (Frederick Warne & Co.), *Wild Wales* (J. M. Dent & Co.), by Theodore Watts-Dunton. Article in Chambers's *Cyclopedia of English Literature*. "Reminiscences of George Borrow" (*Athenæum*, Sept. 3, 10, 1881).

HENRY D. THOREAU (1817–62).

Thoreau, his Life and Aims, by H. A. Page (Chatto & Windus). *Thoreau*, by H. S. Salt ("Great Writers Series"). Essays by R. L. Stevenson (*Familiar Studies of Men and Books*), and J. R. Lowell (*My Study Window*).

The best edition of Thoreau's writings is published by the Riverside Press, Cambridge, U.S.A. Some useful volumes of selections are issued by Walter Scott, Limited, with good introductions by Will. H. Dricks. *Walden*, with introduction by Theodore Watts-Dunton (Henry Froude).

R. L. STEVENSON (1850–94).

Letters of R. L. Stevenson to his Family and Friends (2 vols.), by Sidney Colvin, with introduction. *R. L. Stevenson*, by L. Cope Cornford (Blackwood & Son).

RICHARD JEFFERIES (1848–87).

Eulogy of Richard Jefferies, by Walter Besant (1888). *Nature in Books*, by P. Anderson Graham (Methuen, 1891). *Richard Jefferies*, by H. S. Salt (Swan Sonnenschein, 1894). *Dictionary of National Biography*. Chambers's *Cyclopedia of English Literature*.

WALT WHITMAN (1819–92).

Walt Whitman, by William Clarke (Swan Sonnenschein). Essay by R. L. Stevenson (*Familiar Studies of Men and Books*). *Walt Whitman: a Study*, by J. Addington Symonds. *Walt Whitman*, by R. M. Bucke (Philadelphia). *Walt Whitman*, by John Burroughs (Constable). *The New Spirit* (Essay on Whitman), by Havelock Ellis (Walter Scott). The best edition of *Leaves of Grass*, published by David McKay, Philadelphia.

Footnotes

[0] *The Coming of Love and Other Poems*, by Theodore Watts-Dunton (John Lane).

[21] For an excellent summary of this doctrine, vide *Introduction to Herbert Spencer*, by W. H. Hudson.

[40] *Thomas De Quincey*, by H. S. Salt (Bell's Miniature Biographies).

[48] *De Quincey's Life and Writings*, p. 456, by A. H. Japp, LL.D.

[70] The gypsy word for Antonio.

[71] Devil.

[102] It is a peculiarly American trait. The same thing dominates Whitman. Saxon egotism and Yankee egotism are quite distinctive products.

[106] *Thoreau*, by H. A. Page.

[124a] *Later Essays*.

[124b] Introduction, *The Letters of Robert Lents Stevenson*.

[147] *The Eulogy of Richard Jefferies* by Walter Besant.

[149] Perhaps even more remarkable is the abnormal state of consciousness described in the "Ancient Sage."

[151a] *Six Systems of Indian Philosophy*, by F. Max Müller.

[151b] Quoted by Professor William James, *Varieties of Religions Experiences*, p. 402.

[153a] *Varieties of Religious Experience*, p. 427.

[153b] Vide *Richard Jefferies*, by H. S. Salt.

[157a] *The Life of the Fields*, p. 72.

[157b] Curious similarity of thought here with Elia's "popular fallacy," though probably quite uninspired by Lamb. Jefferies was no great reader. It is said that he knew little or nothing of Thoreau.

[173] *Vide* Introduction to Borrow's *The Romany Rye*, by Theodore Watts-Dunton.

[180] *Familiar Studies of Men and Books*, by R. L. Stevenson.

[186] *Walt Whitman*, a study, by J. A. Symonds.

[188] *Walt Whitman*, by William Clarke, p. 79.

[197] Vide *Life of William Morris* by J. W. Mackail.

[199] *Robert Browning: Essays and Thought*, by John T. Nettleship.

[204] *The New Spirit*, by Havelock Ellis.

Milton Keynes UK
Ingram Content Group UK Ltd.
UKHW030742071024
449371UK00006B/645